Collins

easy learning
English
Conversation 1

The easi
your sp

HarperCollins Publishers
Westerhill Road
Bishopbriggs
Glasgow
G64 2QT

Second edition 2015

10 9 8 7 6 5 4 3 2 1

© HarperCollins Publishers 2011, 2015

ISBN 978-0-00-810174-9

Collins ® is a registered trademark of
HarperCollins Publishers Limited

www.collinsdictionary.com/cobuild
www.collinselt.com

A catalogue record for this book is
available from the British Library

Typeset by Davidson Publishing
Solutions, Glasgow

Audio material recorded and produced
by ID Audio, London

Printed in Great Britain by Clays Ltd,
St Ives plc

Editorial staff

Written by:
Elizabeth Walter and Kate Woodford

Editor: Lisa Sutherland

For the publisher:
Lucy Cooper
Kerry Ferguson
Elaine Higgleton
Celia Wigley

contents

Introduction   5

Units

1   Chatting to people
    The language of conversation   7

2   Travelling
    Travelling around   21

3   Where we live
    Organizing your accommodation   35

4   Eating with friends
    Restaurant conversation   47

5   Going out
    Socializing   61

6   Days out
    Seeing the sights   75

7   Shopping
    Doing some shopping   91

8   Service with a smile
    Dealing with various services   105

9   Health
    Looking after your health   119

10 Help!
    Coping with different problems   131

11 Telephoning and writing
    Making calls, sending emails and letters   145

contents

12 Work
      Speaking with colleagues and customers   161

13 Studying
      Talking about your studies   175

14 Numbers, dates and time
      Everything you need to know   189

Summary of all the phrases by function ...
      A quick reference guide   203

Grammar

      irregular verbs   236
      verb tenses   239
      forming questions   241
      short forms   245
      countable and uncountable nouns   247

Phrasal verbs   251

Collins Easy Learning English Conversation: Book 1 is a completely new type of book for learners of English of all ages. It will help you to be able to speak in natural English, even if you have not been learning English for long.

To sound natural in English, you need to know both the words and the grammar. However, it can be difficult to put these two things together and be sure that what you are saying sounds like natural English. *Collins Easy Learning English Conversation* has been carefully designed to give you whole sentences which you can use with confidence in all your conversations.

Collins Easy Learning English Conversation is made up of 14 units, each giving the language used in a particular situation, for instance shopping, travelling or talking about your health.

In each unit, the language is arranged by language task, for example, 'saying what you want' or 'making suggestions'. Clear headings help you to find what you need. 'Good to know' boxes give advice about things it is important to know.

There are lots of examples of the phrases, and the words in them are explained at the bottom of each page.

At the end of each unit is a page called 'Listen out for', which gives more useful phrases that you may hear or need to use in each situation. This is followed by a conversation, showing the phrases you have learned in a natural situation. You can listen to these conversations on the CD that comes with this book. The CD also contains some useful phrases you can listen to and then practise saying.

After the 14 units, the 'all the phrases by function...' chapter arranges the phrases by language task. So, for example, all the phrases for 'complaining' come together.

After this is a grammar section, giving useful advice on important grammar points, such as how to form tenses, and the differences between countable and uncountable nouns. Finally, there is a short section on useful phrasal verbs.

We hope *Collins Easy Learning English Conversation* will help you speak with confidence and success. For more information on products to help you improve your English, please visit us at **www.collinselt.com**.

Chatting to people

Hello

You will often want to be able to chat with people and get to know them better. The phrases in this unit will help you talk to friends, family, people at work and people that you meet.

Greetings

Use **Hello ...** as a general greeting. It is polite to say **hello** to anyone in any situation.

> **Hello** Jorge.
> **Hello** Dr Ahmed.

Use **Hi ...** in informal situations, for example when you are meeting friends.

> **Hi**, how are things with you?
> Oh **hi** Adam, I didn't know you were coming.

Use **Good morning, Good afternoon** or **Good evening** in slightly more formal situations, for instance if you meet a neighbour, or when you see people at work.

> **Good morning** everyone. Today we are going to be looking at how to form questions.
> **Good afternoon** Mr Kowalski.

> **GOOD TO KNOW!**
> In English, there is no greeting starting with 'Good' that is for the whole day.

Use **Goodbye ...** when you leave someone.

> **Goodbye** Clara, have a safe journey.

Goodbye ... is often shortened to **Bye ...** .

> **Bye** everyone!

Use **Goodnight ...** when you are going to bed, or if someone else is going to bed.

> **Goodnight** everyone – see you in the morning.

See you ... is a rather informal way of saying goodbye to someone you know you will see again.

> OK, I need to go now. **See you!**
> **See you** tomorrow!
> **See you** on Monday!

Introducing people

If you want to introduce someone to someone else, use **This is ...** . To introduce a group of people, use **These are ...** .

> **This is** my husband, Richard.
> **This is** Medina, my friend from school.
>
> **These are** my children, Andrew, Gordon and Emma.
> **These are** my parents.

> **GOOD TO KNOW!**
> When you are introduced to someone, you can just say **Hello**,
> or in a slightly more formal situation, say **Pleased to meet you**.

Useful words

introduce	to tell people each other's names so that they can get to know each other

chatting to people

Talking about yourself

When you are talking to people, you will probably want to tell them some things about you. To say what your name is, use **I'm ...** or, in a slightly more formal situation, **My name's ...** .

> Hi, **I'm** Tariq – I'm a friend of Susi.
> **I'm** Paul – I'm your teacher.

> **My name's** Johann.
> **My name's** Yuko – I'm Kazuo's sister.

If you want to say how old you are, use **I'm ...** . You can just say a number, or you can add **... years old** after the number.

> **I'm** twenty-two.
> **I'm** thirty-seven **years old**.

> **GOOD TO KNOW!**
> We do not usually ask adults their age. If you want to ask a child their age, use **How old are you?** .

To give general information about yourself, use **I'm ...** .

> **I'm** a friend of Paolo's.
> **I'm** married.
> **I'm** interested in old cars.

To talk about your work, use **I'm ...** with the name of a job, or **I work ...** to say something more general about what you do.

> **I'm** a doctor.
> **I'm** a bus driver.

Useful words
an adult	a fully grown person
married	having a husband or wife

I work for an oil company.
I work in Paris.
I work as a translator.

> **GOOD TO KNOW!**
> If you want to ask someone what their job is, use **What do you do?**.

To talk about where you live, use **I live ...** or **I'm from ...** . **I'm from ...**
is also used to talk about where you were born and lived as a child,
even if you do not live there now.

I live in Wales.
We live near Moscow.

I'm from Poland, but I live in Paris now.
We're from Manchester.

> **GOOD TO KNOW!**
> To ask someone where they live, use **Where do you live?** or
> **Where are you from?**.

Asking for information

After saying hello to someone, especially someone we know, we usually ask
about their health, by saying **How are you?** .

Hello, Jan. **How are you?**
It's great to see you, Anna. **How are you?**

> **GOOD TO KNOW!**
> To answer that question, use **I'm fine, thanks.** or **I'm good, thanks.** .
> If you are not well, you could say **Not great, really.** or
> **Not too good, actually.** .

Useful words
a translator   someone whose job is to change words into a different language

To ask someone you know about their life in general, use **How are things?** or **How are things with you?**

> Hello, Jan. **How are things?**
> Nice to see you, Karl. **How are things with you?**

When you are chatting to someone, you will want to ask them about their life. Use **Tell me ...** for general questions.

> **Tell me** about your family.
> **Tell me** a bit about yourself.
> **Tell me** about your work.

To ask someone to describe something, use **What's ... like?**.

> **What's** your course **like?**
> **What's** your home town **like?**
> **What's** your hotel **like?**

You can also use other general question words such as **Where ... ?**, **When ... ?** or **Why ... ?**.

> **Where** is your office?
> **Where** do you work?
> **Where** are you staying?

> **When** did you meet Olga?
> **When** is his party?
> **When** are you going to start your course?

> **Why** did you decide to become a teacher?
> **Why** did you go to Tokyo?
> **Why** did she stop painting?

Saying what you want to do

When you're talking to friends or people at work you will often need to be able to talk about what you would like to do. Use **I'd like to ...** or **I want to ...** .

> **I'd like to** talk to him about Spain.
> **I'd like to** meet your brother.
> **We'd like to** take you out for a meal.

> **I want to** leave by 5 this afternoon.
> **I want to** speak to her as soon as possible.
> **I want to** invite you all for dinner.

Making suggestions

One easy way of making suggestions to your friends and people at work is to use **We could ...** .

> **We could** ask Paul to join us.
> **We could** meet another time.
> **We could** meet at the Café de la Poste.

If you are keen to do something with your friends or people you work with, use **Let's ...** .

> **Let's** stay a bit longer.
> **Let's** invite lots of people.
> **Let's** go to a restaurant later.

Useful words
invite   to ask someone to come to an event

If you want to make a suggestion and see if other people agree with you, use
Shall we ... ? .

> **Shall we** see what Georgi wants to do?
> **Shall we** order a pizza?
> **Shall we** ask Suri if she wants to come with us?

If you have an idea about something you could do, use **How about ... ?** .

> **How about** going swimming?
> **How about** asking for some time off work?
> **How about** sending him a text?

> **GOOD TO KNOW!**
> **How about + -ing**
> The verb that comes after **How about ... ?** must be in the -ing form.

Expressing opinions

When talking to people in a social or work situation, you may want to express
your opinion of something. Use **I think ...** .

> **I think** Sonia's right.
> I really **think** it's too late to go to the cinema.
> **I think** it's a great idea.

If you do not think something is true, use **I don't think ...** .

> **I don't think** Marc's coming.
> **I don't think** we should stay much longer.
> **I don't think** the restaurant is open on Mondays.

If you want to ask other people if they think something is good or bad, use
What do you think of ... ? .

> **What do you think of** his latest movie?
> **What do you think of** this idea?
> **What do you think of** Mira's new boyfriend?

To ask someone if they think something is a good idea, use **What do you think about ... ?** .

> **What do you think about** going out for dinner tonight?
> **What do you think about** inviting Eva?
> **What do you think about** having a party at the weekend?

To agree with someone's opinion, use **I agree.** or **You're right.**. If you want to say who you agree with, use **with**.

> 'This is a great restaurant.' '**I agree**. We often come here.'
> **I agree with** Nigel.
> I completely **agree with** you!

> 'We'll be late if we don't hurry.' '**You're right** — let's go!'
> I think **you're right**.
> Matthieu**'s right**.

If you do not agree with someone, you can use **I don't think so.** .

> 'The food here's lovely, isn't it?' '**I don't think so**. My soup isn't very nice.'
> 'Pierre's really nice, isn't he?' '**I don't think so**. He never speaks to me.'
> 'Travelling by train is really relaxing.' '**I don't think so**. I prefer to fly.'

Useful words
relaxing   making you feel more calm and less worried

Talking about your plans

To tell your friends and people at work about your plans, use **I'm going to ...** .

> **I'm going to** phone him.
> **I'm going to** tell him I can't come.
> **I'm going to** have lunch with Ted.
> **We're going to** meet on Wednesday.

To ask someone about their plans, use **Are you going to ... ?** .

> **Are you going to** go to the concert?
> **Are you going to** look for a new job?
> **Are you going to** get a taxi home?

Making arrangements

To make an arrangement with a friend or someone you work with, use
We can ... .

> **We can** have lunch in town.
> **We can** meet this evening.
> **We can** travel together.

To explain an arrangement, use **I'll ...** .

> **I'll** meet you outside the cinema.
> **I'll** pick you up at seven.
> **I'll** text you when I'm ready.

ful words

eone up   to collect someone from a place

To check if someone is happy with an arrangement, use **Is ... OK?** .

> **Is** eight o'clock **OK?**
> **Is** a pizza **OK?**
> **Is** it **OK** to bring Charlie?

Saying what you have to do

To tell your friends or people at work what you have to do, use **I have to ...** .

> **I have to** make a phone call.
> **I have to** stay in tonight.
> **We have to** be there at eight o'clock.

To ask what someone has to do, use **Do you have to ... ?** .

> **Do you have to** give them an answer today?
> **Do you have to** go now?
> **Do we have to** bring something?

To say what you have to do in a strong way, you can also use **I must ...** .

> **I must** finish this work today.
> **I must** warn them.
> **I must** pay him back this week.

When you want to say that you should or ought to do something, use **I should ...** .

> **I should** call Anne.
> **You should** come and visit us.
> **I should** give you my mobile number.

Useful words
warn   to tell someone about something such as a possible danger
a mobile   a telephone that you can carry wherever you go

● Listen out for

Here are some useful phrases which you may hear or use when you are speaking to friends or people at work.

Have you ever been to Athens?
How long are you staying in Rouen?
Your English is very good.
Are you married?
Have you got any children?
Do you come here often?
Are you enjoying it here?
Have you worked here for a long time?

Do you speak French?
Could you speak more slowly, please?
I'm sorry – I don't understand.
Could you repeat that, please?
Thank you for a lovely evening.
It was lovely to meet you.
I hope we'll see you again some time.

chatting to people

> 🎧 **Listen to the conversation: Track 1**

Katie is at her friend Andrew's party. Scott comes to introduce himself.

A   Hi, I'm Scott. I'm a friend of Andrew's.

B   Oh, pleased to meet you. Andrew has told me a lot about you.

A   You work with him, don't you? What do you do, exactly?

B   I'm a teacher. I teach maths. What about you?

A   I work for an IT company.

B   Oh.... Where are you from?

A   I'm from Brisbane, in Australia.

B   So what do you think of the weather here? It must be cold for you.

A   Well, sometimes Brisbane can be *too* hot, but a bit more sun would be nice!

B   Are you going to stay in this country?

A   I'm not sure. I'd like to travel – maybe to India. But first I should see a bit more of Britain – it's a beautiful country.

B   You're right. There's a lot to see here.

> 🎧 **Listen to more phrases and practise saying them: Track 2**

Travelling

Have a good trip!

If you are travelling, these phrases will help you to find out how to get to places and do things such as buy tickets. They will also help you to talk about travelling in clear, natural English.

Talking about your plans

When you are travelling, you may want to tell people what you will do. For travel plans that you are sure of, use **I'm going to ...** . Use **Are you going to ... ?** to ask someone about their travel plans.

> **I'm going to** spend a day in Madrid.
> **I'm going to** take the train.
> Then **we're going to** go to London.

> **Are you going to** travel together?
> **Are you going to** fly there?

To talk about your plans, you can also use **I plan to ...** .

> **I plan to** spend a few days in Berlin.
> **I plan to** visit some friends.
> **She plans to** work while she's in Australia.

Use **Will you ... ?** to ask if someone is going to do something.

> **Will you** call us when you get there?
> **Will you** take much luggage with you?

Useful words

spend	to use your time doing something
take	to use a vehicle to go from one place to another
fly	to travel somewhere in an aircraft
visit	to go to see someone in order to spend time with them
work	to have a job and earn money for it
luggage	the bags that you take with you when you travel

To talk about something that you would like to do but are not sure that you will do, you can use **I hope to ...** .

> **I hope to** go to Bulgaria this year.
> **I hope to** spend some time in the mountains.
> **We hope to** do a tour of the islands.

To talk about a travel plan that is only possible, use **I might ...** .

> **I might** book a hotel for the night.
> **I might** come home earlier than planned.
> **I might** spend an extra week in Calgary.

Saying what you have to do

If it is important for you to do something while you are travelling, use **I have to ...** or **I need to ...** .

> **I have to** buy a ticket.
> **I have to** take the train to Berlin first.

> **I need to** get to the airport by ten o'clock.
> **We need to** call a taxi.

Useful words

a mountain	a very high area of land with steep sides
a tour	a trip to an interesting place or around several interesting places
an island	a piece of land that is completely surrounded by water
book	to arrange to have or use something, such as a hotel room, at a later time
a hotel	a building where people pay to stay and eat meals
an airport	a place where aeroplanes come and go, with buildings and services for passengers
a taxi	a car that you can hire, with its driver, to take you where you want to go

Another way of **saying** that it is important that you do something is **I must ...** .
This is used especially when it is *very* important that you do something.

> **I must** be back by June 5th.
> **I must** take my passport.
> **You must** take your mobile.

Saying what you want to do

To say what you want to do when you are travelling, use **I'd like to ...** .

> **I'd like to** hire a bike.
> **I'd like to** take the train.
> **I'd like to** change my ticket.

If you know that you do not want to do something, use **I don't want to ...** .

> **I don't want to** travel alone at night.
> **I don't want to** fly, if possible.
> **We don't want to** spend a lot on accommodation.

Making suggestions

If two or more people are trying to decide what to do when travelling,
use **We could ...** or **Shall we ... ?**.

> **We could** take a taxi instead.
> **We could** ask Tobias to take us there.
> **We could** leave tomorrow morning.

Useful words

a passport	an official document that you have to show when you enter or leave a country
a mobile	a telephone that you can carry wherever you go
hire	to pay to use something, such as a car, for a short time
spend	to pay money for things that you want or need
accommodation	buildings or rooms where people live or stay

Shall we travel overnight?
Shall we leave our bags here?
Shall we walk there?

To suggest what someone else can do when they are travelling, use **You could ...** .

You could stay in an apartment in the city.
You could take a boat there.
You could buy a ticket online.

You can use **How about ... ?** if you have an idea about what someone might do.

How about taking an earlier flight?
How about meeting them at the airport?
How about doing a boat trip?

> **GOOD TO KNOW!**
> **How about + -ing**
> The verb that comes after **How about ... ?** must be in the -ing form.

You can also use **Why not ... ?** if you have an idea about what someone might do.

Why not ask Milos to take you?
Why not get up and go early tomorrow morning.
Why not drive there?

Useful words

overnight	happening through the whole night or at some point during the night
an apartment	a set of rooms for living in, usually on one floor and part of a larger building
online	using the Internet
a flight	a trip in an aircraft
a trip	a journey that you make to a particular place and back again
get up	to get out of bed
drive	to control the movement and direction of a car or other vehicle

Asking for information

You may need to go to a particular place or building when you are travelling. Use **Is there ... ?** to ask if there is such a thing where you are. You may need to get someone's attention before you can ask them a question. Use **Excuse me** to do this.

> **Excuse me**, **is there** a garage near here?
> **Is there** a campsite near here?
> **Is there** anywhere with rooms to rent in this village?
> **Is there** a food shop in this street?
> **Are there** any restaurants around here?

You may want to find out the way to do something, for example how to buy a ticket. Use **How do ... ?**.

> Excuse me, **how do** I buy a ticket from this machine?
> **How do** I use this phone?
> **How do** I call a number in Germany?
> **How do** we get to the station?

If you are looking for somewhere and you want information about how to find it, use **Where ... ?**.

> **Where** is the train station?
> Excuse me, **where** is the ticket office?
> **Where** can I buy a ticket?
> **Where** is the town centre?

Useful words

a garage	a place where you can have your car repaired
a campsite	a place where you can stay in a tent
a room	a separate area inside a building that has its own walls
rent	to pay the owner of something in order to be able to use it yourself
a machine	a piece of equipment that uses electricity or an engine to do a particular job
a ticket office	the place in a station that sells tickets

You may need advice when there are many choices and you need to know the right one for you. Ask **Which ... ?**.

> **Which** train do I take, please?
> **Which** bus goes to the town centre?
> **Which** platform is the train for London?
> Excuse me, **which** train goes to Barcelona?

If you want to ask a general question you can use **Is it ... ?**.

> **Is it** this way?
> **Is it** near here?
> **Is it** far?
> **Is it** on the right?

If you want to know the time that something happens, ask **What time ... ?**.

> **What time** does the train leave?
> **What time** do we get to Brussels?
> **What time** do we arrive in Portland?
> **What time** are we boarding?

If you want to ask how much time something takes, use **How long ... ?**.

> **How long** is the flight?
> **How long** does the journey take?
> **How long** does it take?
> **How long** will it take us to walk there?

Useful words

a bus	a large motor vehicle that carries passengers
a platform	the area in a train station where you wait for a train
far	a long way from somewhere
the right	the side that is towards the east when you look north
board	to get into a train, a ship or an aircraft to travel somewhere
a journey	an occasion when you travel from one place to another

If you want to ask how many times something happens, use **How often do ... ?**.

> **How often do** the trains go?
> **How often do** the trains to Cambridge go?
> **How often do** the buses to Edinburgh go?

If you want to ask about the money that you need to do something, use **How much ... ?**.

> **How much** is a ticket to Beijing?
> **How much** is a return ticket?
> **How much** does it cost to fly there?
> **How much** does it cost to hire a car?

Use **Can I ... ?** to ask if you are allowed to do something.

> **Can I** buy a ticket on the train?
> **Can I** leave my bags here?
> **Can I** change my ticket if I need to?
> **Can I** pay by credit card?

Asking for things

To ask for something, use **Can I have ... ?** or **Could I have ... ?**. To be polite, use **please** at the beginning or end of the question.

> **Can I have** a train timetable, please?
> **Can I have** a ticket to Wellington, please?

> **Could I have** two seats together, please?
> **Could I have** a return ticket to Brighton, please?

Useful words

a return ticket	a ticket for a journey to a place and back again
a credit card	a plastic card that you use to buy something and pay for it later
a timetable	a list of the times when trains, buses or planes arrive and depart
a seat	something that you can sit on

You can also ask for something by using **I'd like ...** . Again, to be polite, use **please** at the end.

>**I'd like** two seats, please.
>**I'd like** a receipt, please.
>**I'd like** an aisle seat, please

If you want to find out if something is available, use **Do you have ... ?**.

>**Do you have** a map of the town centre?
>**Do you have** any smaller cars to hire?
>Excuse me, **do you have** any bus timetables?

If you are asking someone if they can do something for you, you should use **Can you ... ?** or **Could you ... ?**. **Could you ... ?** is slightly more polite and formal than **Can you ... ?**. To be polite, you can use **please** at the beginning or end of these sentences.

>**Can you** take us to the Saint-Antoine hotel, please?
>**Can you** stop here, please?
>Please **can you** show us where it is on the map?

>**Could you** write the address for me, please?
>**Could you** show us where it is?
>**Could you** give me the number, please?
>**Could you** give us directions, please?

Useful words

a receipt	a piece of paper that shows you have received goods or money from someone
an aisle	a long, narrow passage where people can walk between rows of seats
a map	a drawing of a particular area, such as a city or a country, that shows things like mountains, rivers and roads
an address	the number of the building, the name of the street, and the town or city where you live or work
directions	instructions that tell you how to get somewhere

When you ask for something, you can simply name what you want, making sure you finish the sentence with **please**.

> A single to Glasgow, **please**.
> A map of the underground, **please**.
> A window seat, **please**.
> **Three** returns to Montreal, **please**.
> **Two** travel cards, **please**.

Saying what you like, dislike, prefer

You may want to talk about what you like and do not like about travelling. To say what you like, use **I like ...** . To say what you do not like, use **I don't like ...** .

> **I like** these country roads.
> **I like** travelling by train.
> **I like** seeing a different way of life.
> I really **like** being in the mountains with all the snow.

> **I don't like** flying.
> **I don't like** driving on the left.
> **I don't like** being away from my family and friends.
> I like the country very much but **I don't like** the heat.

Useful words

a single	a ticket that you use to travel to a place but not return from it
the underground	in a city, the railway system in which electric trains travel below the ground in tunnels
a window	a space in the wall of a building or in the side of a vehicle that has glass in it
country	land that is away from cities and towns
a way of life	the things that people normally do in a place
snow	soft white frozen water that falls from the sky
the left	the side or direction that is opposite the side that most people write with
the heat	when something is hot

> **GOOD TO KNOW!**
> **like + -ing**
> When **like ...** is followed by a verb, the verb is usually in the -ing form.

To ask what someone else likes, use **Do you like ... ?**.

Do you like this area?
Do you like travelling by yourself?
Do you like driving at night?

If you want to say that you like something very much, use **I really like ...** or **I love ...** .

I really like camping.
I really like seeing other countries.
I really like reading on a train.

I love all the hills in that region.
I love driving through the countryside.
We love all the lakes.

If you want to say that you like one thing more than another thing, use **I prefer ...** .

I prefer staying in hotels.
I prefer to take the motorway.
I prefer driving in the daytime when I can see all the scenery.
I do travel on my own but **I prefer** travelling with other people.

Useful words

an area	a particular part of a town, a country, a region or the world
by yourself	on your own and not with anyone else
camping	staying somewhere in a tent
a hill	an area of land that is higher than the land around it
a region	an area of the country or of the world
a lake	a large area of water with land around it
a motorway	a wide road that allows cars to travel very fast over a long distance
the daytime	the part of the day between the time when it gets light and the time when it gets dark
scenery	the land, water or plants that you can see around you in a country area

● Listen out for

Here are some important phrases you are likely to hear and use when you are travelling.

> Tickets, please.
> Could I see your tickets, please?
> Could you have your tickets ready, please?
> Next stop ...
> This is the 5 :45 to London, stopping at Finsbury Park only.
> A return ticket to Portland, please.
> A single ticket to Aberdeen, please.
> You need to change at Oxford.
> The train for Nice leaves from platform three.
> Do you mind if I sit here?
> Go straight on till you get to the traffic lights.
> Carry on down this road.
> Take the second turning on the left.
> It's opposite the cathedral.
> It's very near.
> You can walk there.
> It's too far to walk.
> It will take you ten minutes to walk there.
> It's three stops from here.

Useful words

ready	prepared
Do you mind ... ?	used to ask someone if you can do something
straight on	continuing in one direction
carry on	to continue to do something
opposite	across from

| 🎧 **Listen to the conversation: Track 3** |

Scott is in the ticket office of a train station, buying his ticket.

A I'd like a single to Manchester, please. I need to be there by midday.

B Right, you need the 8:45 train. That will be £45.00.

A Thank you.

B You have to change at Birmingham.

A Okay. What time does the train arrive in Manchester?

B 11:32.

A Right. Which platform is the train for Manchester?

B Platform 18.

A Where is platform 18?

B It's at the far end of the station.

A Okay, many thanks.

Katie and Jemma are starting to plan a holiday together.

A I like the sun so I want to go somewhere nice and hot.

B Me too. We could go to the south of Spain. I've never been there but it sounds lovely.

A Yes, I love Spain. Shall we have a look online and see what we can find?

B Good idea. The only thing is, I really don't want to fly.

A What about getting the boat over to France and then driving? We could even hire a car and then share the driving between us.

B That would be great. I'd like to stop off in France too.

A Yes, if we have time. Remember, I have to be back here by the beginning of August.

B Oh yes, that's when your course starts, isn't it?

A Yes, but that still leaves three weeks.

B That should be plenty!

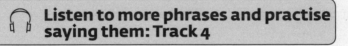

Listen to more phrases and practise saying them: Track 4

Where we live

Make yourself at home!

The phrases in this unit will help you to talk about places to live or to stay when you are away from home. You can use them if you are trying to find a hotel, if you are looking for somewhere to live, or if you want to talk about the place where you live.

Asking for things

To say what you want, use **I'd like ...** .

> **I'd like** a double room.
> **I'd like** to stay three nights.
> **I'd like** a flat near the university.
> **I'd like** a room with a private bathroom.

To talk about the kind of place you want to stay or live, use **I'm looking for ...** .

> **I'm looking for** a room in a shared house.
> **I'm looking for** cheap accommodation in the area.
> **I'm looking for** a place to rent.
> **We're looking for** a house with four bedrooms.

GOOD TO KNOW!
Accommodation is one of the words most often spelled wrong in English. Remember that it has **cc** and **mm**.

Useful words

a double room	a room for two people
a flat	a set of rooms for living in, usually on one floor and part of a larger building
private	only for one particular person or group and not for everyone
share	to have or use something with another person
accommodation	buildings or rooms where people live or stay
rent	to pay the owner of something in order to be able to use it yourself

To explain to someone what you want, use **I want ...** .

> **I want** a house with a large garden.
> **I want** to rent a house for six months.
> **I want** a room with a view of the sea.

If you are in a hotel and you need something, use **Could I have ... ?** .

> **Could I have** the key to my room, please?
> **Could I have** a receipt, please?
> **Could I have** two more towels?

To make sure that a hotel has everything you need, use **Do you have ... ?** .

> **Do you have** internet access?
> **Do you have** a gym?
> **Do you have** any rooms available?

To ask someone to do something for you, use **Could you ... ?** .

> **Could you** show me the room, please?
> **Could you** get someone to repair the window?
> **Could you** call a taxi for me, please?

Useful words

a garden	the part of land by your house where you grow plants
the view	everything that you can see from a place
a receipt	a piece of paper that shows that you have paid for something
a towel	a piece of thick soft cloth that you use to dry yourself
access	when you are able to use equipment
a gym	a large room with equipment for doing physical exercises
available	that you can find or get
repair	to fix something that has been damaged or is not working properly

Talking about yourself

When you are looking for somewhere to live or stay, you may have to talk about yourself. To say what your name is, use **I'm ...** or **My name's ...** .

> **I'm** Gracia.
> Hi, **I'm** Barbara – I've come to look at the room.
>
> **My name's** Alejandro Perez. I've booked a room for tonight.
> Hello, **my name's** Mrs Keane. I'd like to speak to one of your estate agents, please.

To give general information about yourself, use **I'm ...** .

> **I'm** French, but I'm studying here.
> **I'm** very tidy.
> **I'm** the owner of the flat, but I don't live here.

To talk about your work, use **I'm a ...** with the name of a job, or **I work ...** to say something more general about what you do.

> **I'm a** student.
> **I'm a** teacher.
>
> **I work** at the airport.
> **I work** for a transport business.
> **I work** as a translator.

Useful words

book	to arrange to have or use something, such as a hotel room or a ticket to a concert, at a later time
an estate agent	a person whose job is to sell buildings or land
tidy	liking everything to be in its correct place
transport	a system for taking people or things from one place to another in a vehicle
a translator	someone whose job is to say or write things again in a different language

Asking for information

A simple way to ask for information about places to stay or live is to start your sentence with **Is ... ?** .

> **Is** it expensive?
> **Is** it far from the city centre?
> **Is** breakfast included in the price?

To ask if a place has something, use **Is there ... ?**, or **Are there any ... ?** .

> **Is there** a hairdryer in the room?
> **Is there** a TV?
> **Is there** much noise from the neighbours?

> **Are there any** good schools near here?
> **Are there any** rules about having guests to stay?
> **Are there any** more blankets?

You could also use **Does ... have ... ?** .

> **Does** the flat **have** central heating?
> **Does** the hotel **have** a swimming pool?
> **Does** it **have** a garden?
> **Does** it **have** anywhere to park?

Useful words	
expensive	costing a lot of money
include	to have something as one part
a hairdryer	a machine that you use to dry your hair
a neighbour	someone who lives near you
a guest	someone who you invite to your home
a blanket	a large, thick piece of cloth that you put on a bed to keep you warm
central heating	a heating system that uses hot air or water to heat every part of a building
park	to stop a vehicle and leave it somewhere

You can ask questions using **What ... ?** or **Where ... ?** .

What's the name of the hotel?
What's the average price of a flat in this area?
What's the landlord's address?

Where's the bar?
Where is the best area to live?
Where are the lifts?

To ask about time, use **What time ... ?** .

What time's dinner?
What time do you lock the doors at night?
What time do we have to leave in the morning?

To ask about prices, use **How much ... ?** .

How much is a double room per night?
How much rent do you pay?
How much do you charge for breakfast?

Useful words

average	the normal amount for a particular group
a landlord	a man who owns a building and allows people to live there in return for rent
a lift	a machine that carries people or things up and down in tall buildings
lock	to close a door or a container with a key
rent	the money you pay to the owner of something to be able to use it yourself
charge	to ask someone to pay money for something

Asking for permission

If you are staying in a hotel or renting somewhere to live, you may need to ask for permission. You can use **Can I ... ?** .

>**Can I** see the room?
>**Can I** pay by credit card?
>**Can we** use the pool?
>**Can we** camp here?

To check if you can do something, use **Am I allowed to ... ?** .

>**Am I allowed to** use the washing machine?
>**Am I allowed to** have guests?
>**Are we allowed to** bring our dog?

To make sure you will not upset someone, use **Do you mind if ... ?** .

>**Do you mind if** I park my car here for a moment?
>**Do you mind if** leave my suitcase here for five minutes?
>**Do you mind if** we look at the rooms before we decide?

You can also use **Is it OK to ... ?** . This is slightly informal.

>**Is it OK to** use the cooker?
>**Is it OK to** play my guitar?
>**Is it OK to** use my own bedclothes?

Useful words

a credit card	a plastic card that you use to buy something and pay for it later
a pool	a place where people can swim
camp	to stay somewhere in a tent
a washing machine	a machine that you use to wash clothes in
a suitcase	a case for carrying your clothes when you are travelling
a cooker	a piece of kitchen equipment that is used for cooking food
a guitar	a musical instrument with strings
bedclothes	the covers that you use on a bed

Saying what you like, dislike, prefer

To talk about what you like, use **I like ...** .

> **I like** small hotels.
> **I like** campsites in the mountains.
> **I like** this guest house.

If you like something very much, use **I really like ...** or **I love ...** .

> **I really like** living here.
> **I really like** your sofa.
> **I really like** being so close to my work.

> **I love** modern furniture.
> **I love** the peace of the countryside.
> **I love** living on my own.

> **GOOD TO KNOW!**
> **Like/Love + -ing**
> When **like ...** or **love ...** is followed by a verb, the verb is usually in the -ing form.

If you do not like something, use **I don't like ...** .

> **I don't like** this hotel.
> **I don't like** living with my brother.
> **I don't like** this style of building.

Useful words

a campsite	a place where you can stay in a tent
a guest house	a small hotel
a sofa	a long, comfortable seat with a back, and usually with arms, that two or three people can sit on
peace	the state of being quiet and calm
countryside	land that is away from cities and towns

If you want to say that you like one thing more than another, use **I prefer ...** . If you want to talk about the thing you like less, use **to** before it.

> **I prefer** youth hostels **to** camping.
> **I prefer** living alone.
> **I prefer** this town **to** my home town.

Talking about your plans

When you are talking about your plans for where you're going to live or stay, use **I'm going to ...** .

> **I'm going to** stay in Biarritz.
> **I'm going to** rent a cottage in the mountains.
> **We're going to** camp.

You can also use **I'll** plus a verb in the infinitive.

> **I'll be** staying for a week.
> **I'll pay** the rent in advance.
> **We'll arrive** in the evening.

You can tell people about your plans using **I'm planning to ...** .

> **I'm planning to** buy a flat near the river.
> **I'm planning to** rent a room in a colleague's house.
> **I'm planning to** move to London.

Useful words

a youth hostel	a cheap hotel for young people
a cottage	a small house, usually in the country
in advance	before a particular date or event
a colleague	a person someone works with
move	to go to live in a different place

Complaining

You may need to complain about the place where you are staying or living.
A simple way to start a sentence explaining what is wrong is with **It's …** .

> **It's** very cold in my room.
> **It's** too expensive.
> **It's** not big enough.

To talk about something that should not be in the place where you are
living or staying, use **There's …** .

> **There's** too much noise.
> **There's** dirt all over the floor.
> **There's** a damp patch on the wall.

If you think you should have something that you do not have, use **There isn't …** .

> **There isn't** any hot water.
> **There isn't** anywhere to keep my bike.
> **There isn't** enough room to study.

If something is not good enough, use **I'm not happy with …** .

> **I'm not happy with** the food.
> **I'm not happy with** my room.
> **I'm not happy with** the way the place is cleaned.

Useful words

damp	slightly wet
a patch	a part of a surface that is different in appearance from the area around it

● Listen out for

Here are some useful phrases you may hear when you are finding somewhere to stay or live.

What type of accommodation are you looking for?
Whose name is the booking in?
For how many nights?
For how many people?
Breakfast is included in the price.
Can I see your passport, please?
We're full.
There's a 300 euro deposit.
What number can we contact you on?
We don't allow dogs.
How would you like to pay?
Please fill in this form.
Please sign here.
Can you spell your name for me, please?

Useful words

a booking	an arrangement to have a hotel room, tickets, etc. at a particular time in the future
a deposit	a sum of money that is part of the full price of something, and that you pay when you agree to buy it
contact	to telephone someone or send them a message or letter
fill something in	to write information in the spaces on a form
a form	a piece of paper with questions on it and spaces where you should write the answers
sign	to write your name on a document
spell	to write or speak each letter of a word in the correct order

> **Listen to the conversation: Track 5**

It's Scott's first day in his new job at an IT company in Edinburgh. He's having coffee with his new colleague Laura.

A I hope you'll enjoy living in Edinburgh, Scott. It's a great city. Have you found somewhere to live yet?

B No, I'm staying in a cheap hotel at the moment, but I'm looking for a room in a shared house.

A Oh, wouldn't you prefer to live alone?

B No, I thought it'd be a good way to make friends, at least at first.

A Well, actually, there is a spare room in the house where I live. It's a big house – there are five of us there. You could come and have a look, if you like.

B Thanks very much. What's the house like? Does it have central heating? I've heard the winters here are rather cold!

A Oh, yes, don't worry – it's a modern house and it's very warm and comfortable.

B Are there any rules about having guests to stay? My brother will probably come over in the summer.

A That's fine – we all have guests sometimes. It's a very friendly house. I really like living there.

B Could I have a look at the room this evening?

A Sure, I'll give you the address.

> **Listen to more phrases and practise saying them: Track 6**

Eating with friends

Enjoy your meal!

If you are going out for a meal, you will need to make arrangements with your friends about when and where to meet. You will also want to order food and perhaps tell your friends what food you like and do not like. The phrases in this unit will help you to do all this with confidence.

Making arrangements

To suggest a plan to a friend, use **We can ...** .

> **We can** have a coffee somewhere.
> **We can** have dinner in town.
> **We can** have lunch together sometime.
> **We can** eat out.

To say that you will do something as part of that plan, use **I'll ...** .

> **I'll** meet you in the café.
> **I'll** meet you outside the restaurant.
> **I'll** be inside the restaurant.
> **I'll** get to the restaurant for seven o'clock.

To ask someone about the place they want to meet, use **Where ... ?**.

> **Where** shall we meet?
> **Where** shall we go to eat?
> **Where** would you like to eat?

Useful words

a meal	an occasion when people sit down and eat
order	to ask for food and drinks to be brought to you in a restaurant
dinner	the main meal of the day, usually served in the evening
lunch	the meal that you have in the middle of the day
eat out	to eat in a restaurant

To ask someone about the time they want to meet, use **When ... ?** or
What time ... ?.

> **When** shall we eat?
> **When** do you want to meet for dinner?
> **When** do you want to have dinner?

> **What time** shall we meet?
> **What time** would you like to meet?
> **What time** would you like to eat?

To make sure someone is happy with a plan, use **Is ... OK?**.

> **Is** seven o'clock **OK**?
> **Is** an Italian meal **OK** with you?
> **Is** it **OK** to come a bit later?
> **Is** it **OK** to meet in the restaurant?

To ask what the best arrangement is, use **Is it better to ... ?**.

> **Is it better to** meet outside the restaurant?
> **Is it better to** book a table?
> **Is it better to** arrive early?
> **Is it better to** go to a restaurant that we know?

Asking for information

To ask about the place that you are going to, use **Where is ... ?**.

> **Where is** the restaurant?
> Excuse me, **where are** the toilets?

Useful words

late	after the time that something should start or happen
book	to arrange to have or use something, such as a table in a restaurant, at a later time
early	before the usual time

To ask about the price of something, use **How much ... ?**.

> **How much** is a bottle of water?
> **How much** is it for a pizza?
> **How much** is it for three courses?

Use **What is ... ?** to ask about a particular dish.

> **What is** "gravy"?
> Excuse me, **what is** "jelly"?

Use **What is in ... ?** to ask about the foods that are in a particular dish.

> **What is in** this dish?
> **What's in** a "stew"?

Use **Is there any ... ?** or **Are there any ... ?** to ask whether a particular food is in a dish.

> **Is there any** milk in this dessert?
> **Are there any** nuts in this dish?

Useful words

a course	one part of a meal
a dish	food that is prepared in a particular way
gravy	a sauce that is made from the juices that come from meat when it cooks
jelly	a soft sweet food made from fruit juice and sugar that moves from side to side when you touch it
a stew	a meal that you make by cooking meat and vegetables in a liquid
a dessert	something sweet that you eat at the end of a meal
a nut	a dry fruit with a hard shell

Asking for things

When you arrive at the restaurant, you will want to tell the waiter or waitress how many people will be eating so they can find the right size table for you. Use **A table for ... please**.

> **A table for** two, **please**.
> '**A table for** six, **please**.' 'Certainly, Sir.'

In most restaurants, someone will soon come to your table to take your order. To say which dish you want, use **I'd like ...** or **I'll have ...** . To be polite, use **please** after this.

> **I'd like** the Margarita pizza, please.
> **I'd like** the pizza too, please.
> For my starter, **I'd like** the salad, please.
> For my main course, **I'd like** the pasta.
> For dessert, **I'd like** ice-cream.

> **I'll have** the lamb, please.
> **I'll have** the salad as a starter, please.
> For my main course **I'll have** the fish soup.
> For dessert, **I'll have** the fruit.
> **We'll have** water to drink.

> **GOOD TO KNOW!**
> If the waiter or waitress comes to your table to take your order and you have not decided what to choose, say **We haven't decided yet.** or **Could you come back in five minutes, please?**.

Useful words

a waiter	a man whose job is to serve food in a restaurant
a waitress	a woman whose job is to serve food in a restaurant
a starter	a small amount of food that you eat as the first part of a meal
a salad	a mixture of food, usually vegetables, that you usually serve cold
a main course	the biggest part of a meal
pasta	a type of food made from a mixture of flour, eggs and water that is made into different shapes and then boiled
a soup	a liquid food made by boiling meat, fish or vegetables in water

To ask if something is available, use **Do you have ... ?**.

> **Do you have** a children's menu?
> **Do you have** a table outside?

If the waiter or waitress has brought food to your table but you need something else, use **Can I have ... ?** or **Could I have ... ?**. To be polite, use **please** at the beginning or end of the question.

> **Can I have** some more bread, please?
> **Can I have** the dessert menu, please?
> **Can I have** some pepper, please?
> **Can I have** some ketchup, please?

> **Could I have** another fork, please?
> **Could I have** some water, please?
> **Could we have** a bigger table, please?
> **Could I have** the bill, please?

If you are asking someone if they can do something for you, use **Can you ... ?** or **Could you ... ?**. **Could you ... ?** is slightly more polite and formal than **Can you ... ?**. To be polite, use **please** at the beginning or end of these sentences.

> **Can you** pass me the salt, please?
> **Can you** close the window, please?
> **Can you** bring another glass, please?
> Please **can you** bring us some more water?

Useful words

a menu	a list of the food and drink that you can have in a restaurant
outside	not in a building but very close to it
pepper	a spice with a hot taste that you put on food
ketchup	a thick red sauce made from tomatoes
a fork	a tool with long metal points used for eating food
the bill	a document that shows how much money you must pay for something
pass	to give an object to someone
salt	a white substance that you use to improve the flavour of food

Could you take our order, please?
Could you bring us our coffee, please?
Could you bring us the bill, please?
Could you take our plates away, please?

Saying what you want to do

To say what you want to do, use **I'd like to ...** .

I'd like to book a table, please.
I'd like to try that new Spanish restaurant on Green Street.
I'd like to see the dessert menu.
We'd like to order desserts, please.
We'd like to pay by card.

Saying what you like, dislike, prefer

When you are eating in a restaurant, you may like to talk about the food that you like and do not like. To talk about food that you like, use **I like ...** and to ask someone if they like something, use **Do you like ... ?**.

I like cheese.
I like all vegetables.

Do you like fish?
Do you like spicy food?
Do you like Thai food?

Useful words

an order	the thing that someone has asked for
a plate	a flat dish that is used for holding food
a card	a small piece of plastic that you use to pay for things
cheese	a solid food made from milk which is usually yellow or white
a vegetable	a plant that you can cook and eat
spicy	strongly flavoured with spices

If you like something, but not in a strong way, use **I quite like ...** .

>**I quite like** ice-cream.
>**I quite like** burgers.

If you like something very much, you can say **I really like ...** or **I love ...** .

>**I really like** Japanese food.
>**I really like** meat.

>**I love** seafood.
>**I love** desserts.

To tell someone that you do not like a food, use **I don't like ...** .

>**I don't like** olives.
>**I don't like** hot food.
>**I don't like** fast food.

To ask someone if they do not like a particular food, use **Don't you like ... ?**.

>**Don't you like** sweet food?
>**Don't you like** chocolate?

Useful words

a burger	meat that is cut into very small pieces and pressed into a flat, round shape, often eaten between two slices of bread
meat	the part of an animal that people cook and eat
seafood	fish and other small animals from the sea that you can eat
an olive	a small green or black fruit with a bitter taste
hot	having a strong, burning taste
fast food	hot food that is served quickly in a restaurant
sweet	containing a lot of sugar
chocolate	a sweet brown food made from cocoa

To say very strongly that you do not like a food, use **I hate ...** .

> **I hate** mushrooms.
> **She hates** tomatoes.
> **I hate** that flavour.

If you want to say that you like one food more than another, use **I prefer ...** .
If you want to talk about the food you like less, use **to** before it.

> I don't really like meat. **I prefer** fish.
> **I prefer** my wife's food **to** any restaurant food.

Asking for suggestions

If you want to ask the waiter or other people at your table to tell you about
something that is good to eat, use **What do you recommend ... ?**.

> **What do you recommend** as a starter?
> **What do you recommend** for dessert?
> You've been to this restaurant before, Pilar. **What do you recommend**?

To give you an idea about what to eat, you might ask someone at your table
what they have chosen. Use **What are you having ... ?**.

> **What are you having**, Juan?
> **What are you having** for dessert, Yuta?
> **What are you having** for your starter?

Useful words

a mushroom	a plant with a short stem and a round part that you can eat
a tomato	a soft red fruit that you can eat raw in salads or cook like a vegetable
a flavour	the taste of a food or drink

If you want to ask whether you should have or do something, use **Do you think I should ... ?**.

> **Do you think I should** have the tart?
> **Do you think I should** try the snails?
> **Do you think we should** leave a tip?

Making suggestions

One easy way of making suggestions about where to eat and what to eat is to use **We could ...** .

> **We could** eat here, if you like.
> **We could** have coffee with our desserts.
> **We could** just have a salad.

If you are eager to do something, use **Let's ...** .

> **Let's** order a pizza.
> **Let's** ask Neel to join us for dinner.
> **Let's** try that new French restaurant.

If you want to make a suggestion and see if other people agree with you, use **Shall we ... ?**.

> **Shall we** eat now?
> **Shall we** order?
> **Shall we** wait till Maria comes to order?

Useful words

a tart	a case made of flour, fat and water (=pastry) that you fill with fruit or vegetables and cook in an oven
a snail	a small animal with a long, soft body, no legs and a shell on its back
a tip	money that you give to someone to thank them for a job that they have done for you
join	to come together with other people

If you have an idea about something, use **How about ... ?**.

> **How about** finding somewhere to eat in town?
> **How about** sitting outside to eat?
> **How about** sharing a dessert?

GOOD TO KNOW!
How about + -ing
The verb that comes after **How about ... ?** must be in the -ing form.

Talking about your plans

To say what you have decided to eat, use **I'm having the ...** or **I'm going to have the ...** .

> **I'm having the** pie.
> **I'm having the** soup for a starter.

> **I'm going to have the** fish stew.
> **I'm going to have the** pasta for my main course.

If you do not know what to choose, use **I can't decide what to have ...** .

> **I can't decide what to have** for a starter.
> **I can't decide what to have** for a main course.
> There are so many delicious things. **I can't decide what to have**.

If you think you might choose something, use **Perhaps I'll have the ...** .
> **Perhaps I'll have the** salad for my starter.
> **Perhaps I'll have the** salmon for my main course.

Useful words

share	to have or use something with another person
a pie	a dish of fruit, meat or vegetables that is covered with pastry (= a mixture of flour, butter and water) and baked
delicious	very good to eat
salmon	the pink flesh of a large silver fish that people eat

● Listen out for

Here are some useful phrases you may hear in a restaurant.

Do you have a reservation?
I'm sorry, we're full.
This way please.
Follow me please.
Smoking or non-smoking?
Here's the menu.
Are you ready to order?
Can I take your order?
And for you, Sir?
And for you, Madam?
Today's specials are on the board.
I'd recommend the *tarte tatin*.
The pasta comes with a green salad.
Would you like a drink first?
What will you have to drink?
Would you like anything else?
Can I get you anything else?
Is everything all right?
I'll be right with you.
I'll bring it right away.

Useful words

a reservation	a room or a seat that a hotel, a transport company or a restaurant keeps ready for you
full	containing as many people as possible
a special	a dish in a restaurant that is only available on a particular day and is not usually available
a board	a flat piece of wood or plastic that you use for a special purpose
right away	immediately

> 🎧 **Listen to the conversation: Track 7**

Laura and Scott are having a meal in a restaurant. They're deciding what to eat.

A   There's a lot of fish on the menu. Do you like fish, Laura?

B   I do like it but I prefer meat to fish really.

A   I really like fish – I'm going to have the salmon.

B   I can't decide what to have.

A   How about the lamb? That sounds nice.

B   Oh no, it's spicy – I hate spicy food.

A   We could go somewhere else if you prefer?

B   No, I'm sure I'll find something I like. Perhaps I'll have the pasta – ah no, that has olives in it.

A   Don't you like olives?

B   Not really.

A   I love olives – I eat them all the time.

B   You've eaten in this restaurant a few times, haven't you?

A   Sure.

B   Well, what do you recommend?

A   They do really good pizzas. Why not have a pizza?

B   Yes, that's a good idea.

A Okay, shall we order?

B Yes, let's call that waiter over.

> **Listen to more phrases and practise saying them: Track 8**

Going out

Have a good time!

If you are going out, whether it is to a party, a concert or the cinema, these phrases will help you say what you want, ask where things are and ask for what you need.

Making suggestions

One easy way of making a suggestion about where you and a friend can go and what you can do, is to use **We could ...** .

> **We could** go to the park, if you like.
> **We could** go to the theatre, if you like.
> **We could** see a film.

> **GOOD TO KNOW!**
> When people start a sentence with **We could ...** they often add
> **if you like ...** at the end.

If you are eager to do something with someone, use **Let's ...** .

> **Let's** go to the cinema.
> **Let's** buy tickets for Saturday's match.
> I've got a good idea! **Let's** go swimming.

Useful words	
a park	a public area of land with grass and trees, usually in a town, where people go to relax and enjoy themselves
the theatre	the place where you go to see plays or shows
a film	a story that is told using moving pictures on the television or at a cinema
a cinema	a building where people go to watch films
a ticket	a small piece of paper that shows that you have paid to go somewhere or do something
a match	a sports game between two people or teams
swimming	the activity of moving through water by making movements with your arms and legs

Another way to make a suggestion about where to go and what to do is to use **Shall we ... ?**.

> **Shall we** go out for dinner?
> **Shall we** go to a café?
> **Shall we** go out for a walk?

If you have an idea about what to do or where to go, use **How about ... ?**.

> **How about** going somewhere for a coffee?
> **How about** going bowling?
> **How about** taking a picnic to the park?

> **GOOD TO KNOW!**
> **How about + -ing**
> The verb that comes after **How about ... ?** must be in the -ing form.

To suggest what someone else can do or where someone else can go, use **You could ...** .

> **You could** go to a concert.
> **You could** have ice-creams on the terrace.
> **You could** go to a football match.

Useful words

bowling	a game in which you roll a heavy ball down a narrow track toward a group of wooden objects and try to knock down as many of them as possible
a picnic	when you eat a meal outdoors, usually in a park or a forest, or at the beach
a concert	a performance of music
a terrace	a flat area next to a building where people can sit
a match	a sports game between two people or teams

You can also use **Why not ... ?** if you have an idea about what someone else might do.

> **Why not** go to Helena's party?
> **Why not** have a party for him.
> **Why not** invite some friends from work?

Talking about your plans

For a plan that you are sure of, use **I'm going to ...** . Use **Are you going to ... ?** to ask someone about their plan.

> **I'm going to** have a party.
> **I'm going to** go out with some friends tonight.
> **We're going to** have dinner at our friends' house tonight.

> **Are you going to** celebrate now that you've finished your exams?
> **Are you going to** see Ava tonight?
> **Are you going to** invite many people?

You can also use **Will you ... ?** to ask if someone is going to do something.

> **Will you** get a taxi home after the concert?
> **Will you** buy the tickets?
> **Will you** call the box office or shall I?

Useful words

a party	a social event at which people enjoy themselves by doing things like eating or dancing
invite	to ask someone to come to an event
celebrate	to do something enjoyable for a special reason
an exam	a formal test that you take to show your knowledge of a subject
a taxi	a car that you can hire, with its driver, to take you where you want to go
the box office	the place in a theatre where the tickets are sold

To talk about something that you would like to do but are not sure that you will do, you can use **I hope to …** .

> **I hope to** see them in concert.
> **I hope to** have dinner with Gunilla while I'm in Sweden.
> **We hope to** go to the ballet while we're in Moscow.

To talk about a plan that is only possible, use **I might …** .

> **I might** see a band at the weekend.
> **I might** meet up with Farida and Saki tonight.
> **We might** go to a café afterwards.

Asking for information

Use **Is there … ?** or **Are there … ?** to ask if something exists where you are. You may need to get someone's attention before you can ask them this question. Use **Excuse me** to do this.

> Excuse me, **is there** a café near here?
> Excuse me, **is there** a cinema in this part of town?
> **Is there** a football match on this afternoon?

> Excuse me, **are there** any parks in this area?
> Excuse me, **are there** any free concerts on this weekend?
> **Are there** any clubs near here?

Useful words

ballet	a type of dancing with carefully planned movements
a band	a group of people who play music together
meet up	to come together with people
free	used for describing things that you do not have to pay for

If you are looking for something and you want information about how to find it, use **Where ... ?**.

> **Where** is the Belgrade Theatre?
> **Where** is the Arts Cinema?
> **Where** can I buy a ticket for the game?

If you want to know the time that something happens, use **What time ... ?**.

> **What time** does the film start?
> **What time** does the concert finish?
> **What time** shall we meet?

To ask how much time something lasts for, use **How long ... ?**.

> **How long** is the film?
> **How long** is the concert?
> **How long** will you be in this café?

If you want to ask about the money that you need to do something, use **How much ... ?**.

> **How much** is it to get in?
> **How much** is a theatre ticket?
> **How much** does it cost to watch the match?

To ask someone whether something is available, use **Do you have ... ?**.

> **Do you have** any tickets left?
> **Do you have** any tickets for tonight's performance.
> **Do you have** any programmes?

Useful words

a game	an occasion when people do an activity or sport in which they try to win
get in	to enter somewhere
left	still there after everything else has gone or been used
a performance	when you entertain an audience by singing, dancing or acting
a programme	a small book or sheet of paper that tells you about a play or concert

Asking for things

To ask for something, use **Can I have ... ?** or **Could I have ... ?**. To be polite, use **please** at the beginning or end of the question.

> **Can I have** two tickets for the show, please?
> **Can I have** a concert programme, please?

> **Could I have** a cola, please?
> **Could I have** a taxi for 7 Malvern Street?

Another way of asking for something is **I'd like ...** .

> **I'd like** an orange juice, please.
> **I'd like** a ticket for the Rouen-Cherbourg match.
> **I'd like** three tickets, please.

If you are asking someone if they can do something for you, use **Can you ... ?** or **Could you ... ?**. **Could you ... ?** is slightly more polite and formal than **Can you ... ?**. To be polite, use **please** at the beginning or end of these sentences.

> **Can you** tell me where the toilets are, please?
> **Could you** take me to Regent Square, please?

Useful words

show	a performance in a theatre
cola	a sweet brown drink with bubbles in it
an orange	a round, juicy fruit with a thick, orange-coloured skin
juice	the liquid from a fruit or a vegetable

Saying what you like, dislike, prefer

To talk about things you like, use **I like ...** and to ask someone if they like something, use **Do you like ... ?**.

I like going to see bands play.
I like going out with my friends.
He likes dance music.

Do you like dancing?
Do you like horror films?
Do you like eating out?

> **GOOD TO KNOW!**
> **like + -ing**
> When **like ...** is followed by a verb, the verb is usually in the -ing form.

If you like something, but not in a strong way, use **I quite like ...** .

I quite like going to the cinema.
I quite like the theatre.

If you like something very much, you can say **I really like ...** or **I love ...** .

I really like having picnics in the park in the summer.
I really like going to the opera.

I love musicals.
I love having dinner with my friends.
I love being able to walk home.

Useful words

dancing	the activity of moving your body to music
a horror film	a film that is intended to frighten you
eat out	to eat in a restaurant
an opera	a play with music in which all the words are sung
a musical	a play or a film that uses singing or dancing in the story

To tell someone what you do not like, use **I don't like ...** .

> **I don't like** football.
> **I don't like** going to the theatre.
> **I don't** really **like** science fiction films.

To say very strongly that you do not like something, use **I hate ...** .

> **I hate** opera.
> **I hate** being in a crowd.
> I absolutely **hate** noisy clubs.

> **GOOD TO KNOW!**
> **Hate + -ing**
> When **hate ...** is followed by a verb, the verb is usually in the -ing form.

If you want to say that you like one thing more than another, use **I prefer ...** .
If you want to talk about the thing you like less, use **to** before it.

> **I prefer** going to the cinema **to** watching DVDs at home.
> **I prefer** having dinner at friends' houses **to** eating in restaurants.

Expressing opinions

Use **I thought ...** to give your opinion of a film you have seen, a concert you have been to or something else that you have done.

> **I thought** it was a really good film.
> **I thought** the play was a bit long.
> **I thought** it was an excellent concert.

Useful words

science fiction	stories in books, magazines and films about things that happen in the future or in other parts of the universe
a crowd	a large group of people who have gathered together
noisy	making a lot of loud or unpleasant noise
excellent	extremely good

If you want to ask other people if they think something is good or bad, use **What did you think of ... ?**.

> **What did you think of** the band?
> **What did you think of** her voice?
> **What did you think of** the meal?

You can also ask someone for their opinion by saying **What's your opinion of ... ?**.

> **What's your opinion of** her latest film?
> **What's your opinion of** the new club that has just opened on Kings Lane?

To agree with someone's opinion, use **I agree**. If you want to say who you agree with, use **with**.

> 'This is a really cool nightclub.' '**I agree.**'
> **I agree with** Francine. It's a fantastic restaurant.
> I completely **agree with** you. It was a terrible match.

You can also use **You're right ...** to agree with what someone has said.

> '**You're right** – she can't sing!'
> I think **you're right**. His last film was much better.
> Luca**'s right**. The food here is great.

Useful words

your voice	the sound that comes out from your mouth when you speak or sing
a meal	the food that you have on one occasion
cool	fashionable and interesting
a nightclub	a place where people go late in the evening to dance
fantastic	very good
terrible	very bad
sing	to make music with your voice

If you do not agree with someone, you can use **I disagree**. If you want to say who you disagree with, use **with**.

> 'I think the nightlife in the city has really improved.' 'I'm afraid **I disagree**.'
> I'm afraid **I disagree with** you there.
> **I disagree with** Martine. There's very little for young people to do in the evening in this village.

> **GOOD TO KNOW!**
> When people say **I disagree** they often start by saying **I'm afraid** to make their opinion sounds slightly less strong.

You can also use **I don't think so** to disagree with someone.

> 'The show is too long.' '**I don't think so**. I enjoyed it from beginning to end.'
> 'That restaurant has really improved.' '**I don't think so**. I had a really bad meal there a month ago.'
> 'It's the best club in town.' '**I don't think so**. I much prefer Dino's.'

Asking for permission

If you need to ask if you can do something when you are out, the simplest way is to use **Can I ... ?**.

> **Can I** sit anywhere?
> **Can I** pay by card?
> **Can I** take this chair?
> **Can we** sit outside?

Useful words
nightlife	entertainment at night, for example nightclubs
improve	to get better
a village	a very small town in the countryside

If you want to make sure that someone will not be unhappy or angry if you do something, use **Do you mind if ... ?**.

> **Do you mind if** I get to the restaurant later?
> **Do you mind if** I join you?
> **Do you mind if** we sit here?

You can also use **Is it OK ... ?**. This is slightly informal, but you can use it in most situations.

> **Is it OK** to take my mobile in with me?
> **Is it OK** to leave my bag here?
> **Is it OK** to eat inside the cinema?

To ask if something is allowed, use **Are we allowed to ... ?**.

> **Are we allowed to** take pictures?
> **Are we allowed to** speak during the performance?

Useful words

join	to come together with other people
a mobile	a telephone that you can carry wherever you go

● **Listen out for**

Here are some important phrases that are connected with going out.

Are you free tomorrow night?
What are you doing tonight?
Would you like to go out?
How about next week?
I'm afraid I'm busy.
I'm busy next week.
I'd love to.

Where would you like to sit?
Smoking or non-smoking?
Can I see your tickets, please?
Would you like to buy a programme?

Let me get you a drink.
Did you have a good time tonight?
Thank you for inviting me.
It was a great party.
We really enjoyed the party.

Useful words

free	not doing anything else and so able to do something
busy	already doing something, so that you are not free to do something else
great	very good

> 🎧 **Listen to the conversation: Track 9**

Friends Katie and Jemma are deciding what to do tonight.

A I've got an idea. Let's go to the cinema.

B Do you know what's on?

A Well, there's the new James Daniels film. We could go and see that.

B I don't really like his films. They're too long.

A I disagree – but we don't have to see a film if you don't want to. What about going bowling?

B Ah, yes, I haven't been bowling for ages. That would be fun.

A Is it OK if I invite Ingrid?

B Sure – good idea. How about inviting Riku too? It would be nice to see them both.

A Oh, okay, shall I call them?

B Yes, why not?

A Is there a café near the bowling alley? We could meet them for a coffee first.

B Yes, there's a café just next to it. Why not meet them there?

A Okay, I'll suggest that to them. What time shall we say?

B What about five o'clock inside the café?

A That sounds good. I'll see what they say.

> 🎧 **Listen to more phrases and practise saying them: Track 10**

Days out

Have a nice day!

If you are visiting a city or a part of a country, these phrases will help you say what you want, ask where things are and ask for what you need.

Saying what you want to do

To say what you want to do, use **I'd like to ...** .

I'd like to go to the museum.
I'd like to go up the church tower.
We'd like to see the art exhibition.

If you are very eager to do something, use **I'd really like to ...** or **I'd love to ...** .

I'd really like to see the Great Wall of China.
I'd really like to take the children to the beach.
I'd really like to take some photos of the town.

I'd love to go to the cinema.
I'd love to go walking in the mountains.
I'd love to visit the palace.

Useful words

a museum	a building where you can look at interesting and valuable objects
a tower	a tall, narrow building, or a tall part of another building
an exhibition	a public event where art or interesting objects are shown
a beach	an area of sand or stones next to a lake or the sea
a palace	a very large and impressive house where a king, a queen or a president lives

Talking about your plans

We often say **I'm going to ...** or **I'll** plus an infinitive verb to talk about what we will do in the future.

> **I'm going to** visit the palace of Versailles.
> **I'm going to** phone to find out if it's open on Sundays.
> **We're going to** take the children with us.

> **I'll** meet you by the cathedral at 12 o'clock.
> **I'll** go to the Picasso museum first.
> **We'll** take a train to Berlin.

Use **Are you going to ... ?** or **Will you ... ?** to ask someone about their plans.

> **Are you going to** buy a guidebook?
> **Are you going to** visit the Acropolis?
> **Are you going to** take a picnic with you?

> **Will you** spend all day at the museum?
> **Will you** have time to see the gardens?
> **Will you** take your camera with you?

Useful words

find something out	to learn the facts about something
a cathedral	a large and important church
a guidebook	a book for tourists that gives information about a town, an area or a country
a picnic	a meal that you eat outdoors
spend	to use your time doing something

Making suggestions

If two or more people are trying to decide what to do, use **We could ...** or **Shall we ... ?**.

> **We could** go to the zoo.
> **We could** take a ferry to the island.
> **We could** take him to the science museum.

> **Shall we** go to the beach?
> **Shall we** go to the disco?
> **Shall we** try and climb to the top?

To suggest what someone else can do, use **You could ...** .

> **You could** go on a tour of the city.
> **You could** ask Janne to show you the old town.
> **You could** take the children to the fair.

Use **How about ... ?** if you have an idea about what to do.

> **How about** taking a boat trip round the harbour?
> **How about** doing a tour of the football stadium?
> **How about** going to the Picasso museum?

GOOD TO KNOW!
How about + -ing
The verb that comes after **How about ... ?** must be in the -ing form.

Useful words

a zoo	a park where animals are kept and people can go to look at them
a ferry	a boat that regularly takes people or things a short distance across water
an island	a piece of land that is completely surrounded by water
a disco	a place or an event where people dance to pop music
a tour	a trip around an interesting place
a harbour	an area of water next to the land where boats can safely stay
a stadium	a large sports pitch with rows of seats all around it

Asking for information

When you are asking for information you may need to get someone's attention before you can ask them a question. To do this, first say **excuse me**.

>**Excuse me**, is the modern art museum near here?
>**Excuse me**, do you know what time the gardens open?
>**Excuse me**, where do I buy a ticket?

Use **Is ... ?** to ask general questions about things.

>**Is** the castle interesting?
>**Is** the museum free or do you have to pay?
>**Is** it far to the ice rink?

Use **Is there ... ?** or **Are there any ... ?** to ask whether something exists.

>Excuse me, **is there** a tourist information office near here?
>**Is there** much to do in Liverpool?
>**Is there** somewhere to leave our coats?

>**Are there any** cheaper tickets?
>**Are there any** activities for children?
>**Are there any** good walks around here?

To ask about the time, use **What time ... ?**

>**What time** does the park close?
>**What time** is the next guided tour?
>**What time** do I need to be there?

Useful words

a castle	a large building with thick high walls that was built in the past to protect people during wars and battles
an ice rink	a place where people go to skate (= move over ice on special shoes)
a tourist	a person who is visiting a place on holiday
an activity	something that you spend time doing
a guided tour	a trip around an interesting place with someone who tells you about it

To ask about the price of something, use **How much ... ?**

> **How much** is this postcard, please?
> **How much** is a student ticket?
> **How much** are the tickets?

To ask about the time that something will take, use **How long ... ?**

> **How long** does the tour last?
> **How long** is the boat trip?
> **How long** does it take to get there?

To ask how to do something, use **How do you ... ?**

> **How do you** get to the old town?
> **How do you** buy tickets?
> **How do you** know which bus to catch?

> **GOOD TO KNOW!**
> **How do you + infinitive**
> The verb that comes after **How do you ... ?** must be in the infinitive without 'to'.

Asking for things

To ask for something, use **Can I have ... ?** or **Could I have ... ?**. To be polite, use **please** at the beginning or end of the question.

> **Can I have** two tickets, please?
> **Can I have** your guidebook for a minute?
> **Can I have** an audio guide, please?

Useful words

a postcard	a thin card, often with a picture on one side, that you can write on and post to someone without using an envelope
catch	to get on a bus, train or plane in order to travel somewhere
an audio guide	a piece of equipment that gives you spoken information about a place

Could I have two tickets, please?
Could I have a programme for this evening's concert?
Could I have three seats together?

Another way of asking for something in a shop is **I'd like ...** .

I'd like a map of the area, please.
I'd like two tickets for 'Oliver'.
I'd like seats in the front row, if possible.

If it is important for you to have something, you can use **I need ...** .

I need the address of the museum.
She needs two more tickets.
I need a street map of the city.
We need a guide who can speak English.

If you want to ask if something you want is available, use **Do you have ... ?** .

Do you have any brochures in English?
Do you have any information on trips in this area?
Do you have tickets for tomorrow's show?

Useful words

a programme	a small book or piece of paper that tells you about a play or concert
a row	a line of seats
an address	the number of the building, the name of the street, and the town or city where a building is
a guide	someone who shows tourists around places such as museums or cities
a brochure	a thin magazine with pictures that gives you information about a place, a product or a service
a show	a performance in a theatre

If you are asking someone if they can do something for you, use **Can you ... ?** or **Could you ... ?** . **Could you ... ?** is slightly more polite and formal than **Can you ... ?** . To be polite, use **please** at the beginning or end of these sentences.

> **Can you** tell me what the opening hours are?
> **Can you** give me directions to the Science Museum?
> **Please can you** show me where we are on this map?

> **Could you** take me to the old town, please?
> **Could you** check if I've got the right tickets?
> **Could you** tell me the way to the theatre?

Asking for permission

If you need to ask if you can do something, the most simple way is to use **Can I ... ?**.

> **Can I** use this ticket on the bus as well?
> **Can I** take my bag in?
> **Can we** park our car here?

If you want to check that someone will not be unhappy or angry if you do something, use **Do you mind if ... ?** .

> **Do you mind if** I pay later?
> **Do you mind if** we sit on the grass?
> **Do you mind if** I leave the pushchair here?

Useful words

opening hours	the times that a place is open
check	to make sure that something is correct
park	to stop a vehicle and leave it somewhere
a pushchair	a small chair on wheels used for moving a young child around

You can also use **Is it OK ... ?**. This is slightly informal, but you can use it in most situations.

> **Is it OK** to take photos?
> **Is it OK** if we come back later?
> **Is it OK** to bring a friend?

To ask if something is allowed, use **Are we allowed to ... ?** .

> **Are we allowed to** take drinks into the cinema?
> **Are we allowed to** come back in again later?
> **Are we allowed to** ask questions?

Saying what you like, dislike, prefer

To talk about things you like, use **I like ...** and to ask someone if they like something, use **Do you like ... ?**.

> **I like** visiting modern art galleries.
> **I like** outdoor concerts.
> **I like** this sculpture very much.

> **GOOD TO KNOW!**
> **Like + -ing**
> When **like ...** is followed by a verb, the verb is usually in the -ing form.

> **Do you like** going to concerts?
> **Do you like** modern art?
> **Do you like** looking at old churches?

Useful words
outdoor	happening outside and not in a building
a sculpture	a piece of art that is made into a shape from a material like stone or wood

If you like something, but not in a strong way, use **I quite like ...** .

> **I quite like** going to films.
> **I quite like** the ballet.
> **I quite like** exploring new places.

If you like something very much, you can say **I really like ...** or **I love ...** .

> **I really like** going walking with friends.
> **I really like** the harbour area.
> **I really like** relaxing in the park.

> **I love** the small villages of Provence.
> **I love** this type of architecture.
> **I love** this museum.

To tell someone what you do not like, use **I don't like ...** .

> **I don't like** bus tours.
> **I don't like** visiting old ruins.
> **I don't like** Shakespeare.

To say very strongly that you do not like something, use **I hate ...** .

> **I hate** being late.
> **I hate** horror movies.
> **I hate** travelling by underground.

Useful words

ballet	a type of dancing with carefully planned movements
relax	to feel more calm and less worried
architecture	the style of the design of a building
ruins	the parts of a building that remain after something destroys the rest
a horror movie	a very frightening film
underground	a railway system in a city in which electric trains travel below the ground in tunnels

> **GOOD TO KNOW!**
> **Hate + -ing**
> When **hate ...** is followed by a verb, the verb is usually in the -ing form.

If you want to say that you like one thing more than another, use **I prefer ...** .
If you want to talk about the thing you like less, use **to** before it.

> **I prefer** museums **to** religious buildings.
> **I prefer** modern art.
> **I prefer** walking **to** cycling.

Complaining

You may have to complain about something which you're unhappy with. If you are complaining about something that you are doing, use **It's ...** .

> **It's** too crowded.
> **It's** boring.
> **It's** badly organized.

To talk about an event or an activity that is now over, use **It was ...** .

> **It was** really expensive.
> **It was** a waste of money.
> **It was** difficult to find.

Useful words

religious	connected with religion
crowded	full of people
boring	not interesting
organize	to plan or arrange something
a waste of money	when you spend money on something that is not useful or enjoyable

To talk about something that you are not happy with at a place, use **There's ...** .

> **There's** rubbish all over the place.
> **There's** nowhere to park.
> **There's** a lot of building work going on.

To talk about something that a place does not have, use **There isn't ...** .

> **There isn't** anywhere to sit down.
> **There isn't** any information about the paintings.
> **There isn't** room to park.

Useful words
rubbish   objects you do not want any more

● Listen out for

Here are some useful phrases you may hear on your day out.

What language would you like the information in?
Here's a leaflet in English.
Do you have a student card?
The museum's open from nine to three.
The gallery's closed on Sundays.
The next guided tour's at ten.
How many tickets would you like?
It's eight dollars each.
You're not allowed to take pictures.
Can I search your bag?
Please leave your bag and coat in the cloakroom.
Keep off the grass.
Did you enjoy it?

Useful words

a leaflet	a piece of paper containing information about a particular subject
search	to look carefully in a place for something or someone
a cloakroom	a room in a building where you can leave your coat

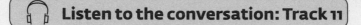

Listen to the conversation: Track 11

Scott is visiting his friend Beth, who lives in London.

A Do you have any plans for today, Scott?

B I'd like to go to St Paul's Cathedral. I really like visiting churches.

A Really? I prefer modern buildings. Do you mind if I don't come with you?

B That's fine.

A How about meeting for lunch afterwards?

B Great idea. What's the best way to get there?

A You can go on the underground.

B How long will it take?

A About twenty minutes.

B Are you allowed to take photos inside the cathedral?

A I think so. OK, have a great morning, and I'll see you later.

Scott is trying to buy tickets to a show for him and Beth.

A Do you have any tickets for 'Les Miserables'?

B Yes, do you want to go this evening?

A What time is the show?

B It starts at 7.30. Is that OK?

A Yes, that's fine. How much are the tickets?

B £65 each.

A **Are there any cheaper seats?**

B There are some for £18 if you have a student card.

A **I'm not a student.**

B Well, there are some nearer the back for £25.

A **OK, I'd like those, please.**

Listen to more phrases and practise saying them: Track 12

Shopping

Can I help you?

The phrases in this section will help you do your shopping. If you need to buy clothes, food, or things for your house, use these phrases.

Asking for things

To ask for something in a shop, use **I'd like ...** or **Could I have ... ?** .

> **I'd like** two kilos of potatoes, please.
> **I'd like** a bottle of water.
> **I'd like** two red peppers.

> **Could I have** a kilo of oranges, please?
> **Could I have** a book of stamps?
> **Could I have** a carrier bag, please?

You can also say what you are looking for by using **I'm looking for ...** or **I need ...** .

> **I'm looking for** a camera for my daughter.
> **I'm looking for** a white shirt.
> **I'm looking for** some plastic cups.
> **I'm looking for** a present for my Mum.

> **I need** a new coat.
> **I need** mozzarella.
> **I need** some batteries for my alarm clock.

Useful words

a pepper	a hollow green, red or yellow vegetable with seeds inside
a carrier bag	a plastic or paper bag with handles that you use for carrying shopping
mozzarella	a type of white Italian cheese
a battery	a small object that provides electricity for things such as radios
an alarm clock	a clock that makes a noise to wake you up

To ask if a shop sells the thing you want, use **Do you sell ... ?** or **Have you got ... ?** .

Do you sell light bulbs?
Do you sell balloons?
Do you sell newspapers?

Have you got any mangoes?
Have you got any large suitcases?
Have you got a doll with long hair?

When you have decided what you want to buy, use **I'll have ...** or **I'll take ...** .

I'll take these two postcards.
I'll take the blue ones.
I'll take two pineapples.

I'll have a strawberry ice cream.
I'll have the red one.
I'll have 200 grams of ham.

Saying what you have to do

If you need to buy something, use **I have to ...** or **I've got to ...** .

I have to buy some new shoes.
I have to go to the baker's.
I have to get some bread.
We have to buy some new chairs.

Useful words

a balloon	a small, thin, brightly-coloured rubber bag that you blow air into so that it becomes larger
a mango	a large, sweet yellow or red fruit that grows in hot countries
a suitcase	a case for carrying your clothes when you are travelling
a doll	a child's toy that looks like a small person or a baby
a pineapple	a large fruit with sweet yellow flesh and thick, brown skin
a strawberry	a small soft red fruit that has a lot of seeds on its skin
ham	meat from a pig that has been prepared with salt and spices
a baker's	a shop where you can buy bread and cakes

I've **got to** buy a present for Max.
I've **got to** get a new toothbrush.
I've **got to** replace my old laptop.

You could also use **I need to ...** .

I need to get some apples.
I need to buy a tent.
I need to get a new pair of glasses.

To talk about some shopping that is very important, use **I must ...** .

I must find a dress for the party on Saturday.
I must find a birthday present for my sister.
I must buy a suit for the interview.

Talking about your plans

To tell someone what you are going to do, use **I'm going to ...** .

I'm going to buy a new pair of trousers.
I'm going to go to the sales this weekend.
We're going to buy a new bed.

Useful words	
a present	something that you give to someone, for example on their birthday
a toothbrush	a small brush that you use for cleaning your teeth
a laptop	a small computer that you can carry with you
a tent	a shelter made of cloth that is held up by poles and ropes, and that you sleep in when you go camping
glasses	two pieces of glass or plastic (= lenses) in a frame, that some people wear in front of their eyes to help them see better
a suit	a jacket and trousers or a jacket and skirt that are both made from the same cloth
an interview	a formal meeting in which someone asks you questions to find out if you are the right person for a job
the sales	a time when a shop sells things for less that their normal price

To talk about what you're thinking of buying or where you're thinking of going, use **I'm thinking of ...** .

> **I'm thinking of** going to the market tomorrow.
> **I'm thinking of** going shopping in Paris.
> **I'm thinking of** buying a new car.

For something you would like to do, but that is not certain, use **I hope to ...** .

> **I hope to** find something for under 20 euros.
> **I hope to** get a cheap sofa in the sales.
> **We hope to** find a present for Miyoko.

Expressing opinions

When you look at things in shops, you may want to say what you think of them. Use **I think ...** or **I don't think ...** .

> **I think** this wardrobe is really beautiful.
> **I think** this shirt would suit you.
> **I think** the mangoes look good.

> **I don't think** this jumper is warm enough.
> **I don't think** the quality of the material is very good.
> **I don't think** the shop assistants are very well trained.

Useful words

a market	a place where people buy and sell products
cheap	costing little money or less than you expected
a wardrobe	a cupboard where you hang your clothes
suit	to make you look attractive
a jumper	a warm piece of clothing that covers the top part of your body
a shop assistant	a person who works in a shop
train	to teach someone the skills they need in order to do something

To agree with someone's else's opinion, use **I agree.** or **You're right.** .

> **I agree** with you that the blue dress is nicer.
> 'These shoes are lovely.' **'I agree** – I'm going to try some on.'
> 'This shop is much too expensive.' ' **I agree** – let's go somewhere else.'

> 'It's too tight around the waist.' **'You're right**. I need a bigger size.'
> 'It's a lot of money to spend on a TV.' **'You're right**, but I want a really good one for the World Cup.'
> 'You don't need another pair of jeans.' **'You're right**.'

If you are shopping with someone else, you may want to ask for that person's opinion about something you are thinking of buying. Use **What do you think ... ?** .

> **What do you think** of these trousers?
> **What do you think** about getting Jack a DVD?
> **What do you think** of this shop?

If you are trying to choose between things in a shop and you want an opinion from the person you are with, use **Which ... ?** .

> **Which** one do you like best?
> **Which** dress shall I buy?
> **Which** skirt fits best?

Useful words

try something on	to put on a piece of clothing to see if it fits you or if it looks nice
tight	small, and fitting closely to your body
waist	the middle part of your body
a skirt	a piece of clothing for women and girls that hangs down from the waist and covers part of the legs
fit	to be the right size for someone or something

Asking for information

For general information, use questions such as **Where ... ?** or **Which ... ?** .

> **Where**'s the nearest bank, please?
> **Where** can I find sunglasses?
> **Where** are the changing rooms?

> **Which** brand do you recommend?
> **Which** batteries do I need to buy for my camera?
> **Which** floor is the children's department on?

If you want to ask if a town has a particular shop, use **Is there ... ?** .

> **Is there** a supermarket near here?
> **Is there** a butcher's in this town?
> **Is there** a car park near the market?

You can also use **Is there ... ?** or **Do you have ... ?** to ask if a shop has something.

> **Is there** an organic food section?
> **Is there** anyone who can help me carry this to the car?
> **Is there** a changing room?

Useful words	
sunglasses	dark glasses that you wear to protect your eyes from bright light
a changing room	a room in a clothes shop where you can try clothes
a brand	the name of a product that a particular company makes
recommend	to suggest that someone would find a particular person or thing good or useful
a butcher's	a shop where you can buy meat
a car park	an area of ground or a building where people can leave their cars for a period of time
organic	grown without using chemicals

Do you have any other saucepans?
Do you have it in a smaller size?
Do you have any trolleys?

To ask for information about something you might buy, use **Is this ... ?** or
Is it ... ? .

Is this the only model you have?
Is this the biggest size?
Are these the only colours you have?

Is it made of real leather?
Is it big enough for four people?
Is it free?

To ask for the price of something, use **How much ... ?** .

How much is a bottle of orange juice?
How much are the tomatoes, please?
How much is this vase?
How much are the batteries?

To ask whether you can do something, use **Can I ... ?** .

Can I pay by credit card?
Can I have it giftwrapped?
Can I have a discount if I buy ten?

Useful words

a saucepan	a deep metal cooking pot, usually with a long handle and a lid
a trolley	a large container with wheels that you use for moving heavy things such as shopping
a model	a particular design on something
leather	animal skin that is used for making shoes, clothes, bags and furniture
a vase	a container that is used for holding flowers
a credit card	a plastic card that you use to buy something and pay for it later
giftwrap	to put coloured paper around something so that it can be given as a present
a discount	a reduction in the usual price of something

Saying what you like, dislike, prefer

To say that you like something, use **I like ...** .

> **I like** this shop.
> **I like** these shoes very much.
> **I like** the cakes they sell here.

To say that you like something very much, use **I really like ...** .

> **I really like** the greengrocer's near the church.
> **I really like** this sofa.
> **I really like** looking for bargains.

If you do not like something, use **I don't like ...** .

> **I don't like** these plates very much.
> **I don't like** big stores.
> **We don't like** queuing.

> **GOOD TO KNOW!**
> **Like + -ing**
> When **like ...** is followed by a verb, the verb is usually in the -ing form.

To say that you like one thing more than another, use **I prefer ...** . If you want to talk about the thing you like less, use **to** before it.

> **I prefer** the green one.
> **I prefer** small shops **to** supermarkets.
> **We prefer** fresh vegetables.
> **I prefer** to buy books on the internet.

Useful words

a greengrocer's	a shop that sells vegetables and fruit
a sofa	a long, comfortable seat with a back, and usually arms, that two or three people can sit on
a bargain	something that is being sold at a lower price than usual
queue	to stand in a line of people that are waiting for something
fresh	picked, caught or produced recently

You can also use **I like ... more than ...** .

> **I like** the pink one **more than** the red one.
> **I like** the plastic cups **more than** the glass ones.
> **I like** orange juice **more than** apple juice.

Making suggestions

If you are shopping with a friend, use **We could ...** or **Shall we ... ?** to make suggestions.

> **We could** have a look in another shop.
> **We could** ask them to order it for us.
> **You could** ask them for a discount.

> **Shall we** buy the fridge today?
> **Shall we** get a present for Joe?
> **Shall we** go to a bigger store?

If you are keen to do something, you could say **Let's ...** .

> **Let's** buy some flowers.
> **Let's** get the expensive one – it will be much better.
> **Let's** choose some new bedclothes.

Useful words

order	to ask for something to be sent to you from a company
a fridge	a large container that is kept cool inside, usually by electricity, so that the food and drink in it stays fresh
bedclothes	the pieces of cloth that cover you in bed

Asking for permission

To ask someone in a shop if you can do something, use **Can I ... ?** .

Can I try on this skirt?
Can I keep the hanger?
Can I bring it back if I don't like it?
Can I change this coat for a different one?
Can my daughter try on this jacket?

A polite way of asking for permission is **Do you mind if I ... ?** .

Do you mind if I open the packet?
Do you mind if I try on another pair?
Do you mind if I taste one of these cherries?

A slightly informal way of asking for permission is **Is it OK to ... ?**.

Is it OK to look inside the box?
Is it OK to try one of your oranges?
Is it OK to take the alarm clock out of its box?

Useful words

a hanger	an object for hanging clothes on
a packet	a small box, bag or envelope in which an amount of something is sold
a cherry	a small, round fruit with red skin
an alarm clock	a clock that makes a noise to wake you up

● Listen out for

Here are some useful phrases you may hear when out shopping.

Are you being served?

Can I help you?

What size are you?

Do you need a smaller size?

Shall I look for a larger size for you?

What colour would you like?

How much were you thinking of spending?

We don't have any in stock just now.

Anything else?

Is it a present for someone?

Shall I giftwrap it for you?

Would you like to keep the hanger?

It's cash only, I'm afraid.

I'm afraid we don't take credit cards.

Could you sign here, please?

How would you like to pay?

Can you put your PIN number in, please?

You can take your card now.

Useful words

in stock	available for you to buy
cash	money in the form of notes and coins

> ## 🎧 Listen to the conversation: Track 13

Katie is shopping for clothes with her friend Jemma.

A I need to get something to wear to Lola's party on Saturday.

B OK, where do you want to look?

A I really like that shop near the river, but it's a bit expensive.

B Let's go there first and have a look. We could go somewhere else afterwards if you can't find anything you can afford.

Katie and Jemma are now in the shop.

A What do you think of this dress?

B It's nice, but I don't think it's suitable for a party - it's a little dull.

A You're right. Let's see if there are any others.

B This one would look nice on you.

A I don't like it – it's too old-fashioned. I'm looking for something more modern. Oh, look – this one's lovely!

B Yeah, I really like the colour.

A They have the same dress in blue – which do you prefer?

B I like the red one more than the blue one. How much is it?

A Oh dear, it's much more than I want to spend.

B Go on, treat yourself! It's the kind of dress you'll wear again and again.

A You're right. I will!

> 🎧 **Listen to more phrases and practise saying them: Track 14**

Useful words

can afford something	to have enough money to pay for something
suitable	right for a particular purpose or occasion
dull	boring
old-fashioned	no longer used, done or believed by most people
silk	a smooth shiny cloth that is made from very thin threads

Service with a smile

Excellent service!

If you need a service of some sort, or need help or information, these phrases will help you say what you want and ask for what you need.

Greetings

Use **Hello ...** as a general greeting to people in shops and banks, etc. It is polite to say **hello** to anyone in any situation.

> **Hello**, Madam.
> **Hello**, I wonder if you can help me.

Use **Hi ...** to greet people in more informal situations, for example a hairdresser's where you know the hairdresser.

> **Hi**, can I make a hair appointment?
> **Hi**, I'm seeing Freya for a haircut at 10:00.

You can use **Good morning, Good afternoon** or **Good evening** in slightly more formal situations, although to some people, this sounds slightly old-fashioned.

> **Good morning**. I'd like some advice on holiday insurance.

> **GOOD TO KNOW!**
> In English, there is no greeting starting with 'Good' that is for the whole day.

Useful words

a hairdresser's	a place where you go to have your hair cut
hair	the fine threads that grow on your head
an appointment	an arrangement to see someone at a particular time
a haircut	an occasion when someone cuts your hair for you
advice	what you say to someone when you are telling them what you think they should do
insurance	an agreement that you make with a company in which you pay money to them regularly, and they pay you if something bad happens to you

Use **Goodbye** when you leave a shop or bank, etc.

> Thanks for all your help. **Goodbye**.

Goodbye is often shortened to **Bye**. **Bye** is slightly informal.

> Thanks very much. **Bye**.

See you ... is a slightly informal way of saying goodbye, for example to a hairdresser that you know you will see again.

> Thanks very much. **See you** soon!
> Thanks, Louisa. **See you** in a couple of months.

People who work in shops often say **Have a good day!** or **Have a good weekend!** as you are leaving.

> Goodbye, **have a good day!**
> Bye, **have a good weekend!**

Talking about yourself

Often you will need to tell people information about yourself, such as your name and where you live. To say what your name is, use **My name is ...** .

> **My name is** Latif Keita.
> **My name is** Astrid Backstrom.
> **My husband's name is** Olivier Dauga.

Useful words

a couple	two or around two people or things
a month	one of the twelve parts that a year is divided into
a weekend	Saturday and Sunday

To say where you live, use **my address is ...** .

> **My address is** 29 Kelvin Close, L3 0QT Liverpool.
> **My address** in New Zealand **is** 20 John Street, Auckland
> **My** permanent **address is** 7 avenue Foch in Aix.

To say which country you were born in and lived in as a child, us **I'm from ...** .

> **I'm from** Algeria.
> **I'm from** Aberdeen in Scotland.
> **We're from** Bulgaria.

To say where you are from, you can also use **I'm ...** .

> **I'm** Canadian.
> **I'm** Norwegian.

You can give other useful information using **I'm ...** .

> **I'm** on holiday.
> **I'm** here for two weeks.
> **I'm** 26.
> **We're** here for three months.

If you want to say that you are living somewhere for a short time, for example because you are on holiday, use **I'm staying ...** .

> **I'm staying** at a hotel.
> **I'm staying** with a host family.
> **We're staying** in a rented house.

Useful words

permanent	continuing forever or for a very long time
be born	to come out of your mother's body and begin life
a host	someone who invites people to stay in their home
rented	used by people who pay money to the owner

Saying what you have to do

To say what service or help you need, you can use **I have to ...** or **I need to ...** .

> **I have to** go to the bank this afternoon.
> **I have to** collect my jacket from the dry-cleaner's.
>
> **I need to** get my camera repaired.
> **I need to** go to the optician's.

To say that you need a particular thing, use **I need ...** .

> **I need** some advice.
> **I need** some information about insurance.

To ask what someone has to do, use **Do you have to ... ?** .

> **Do you have to** speak to someone at the bank?
> **Do you have to** show your passport?

Another way of saying that it is important that you do something is **I must ...** . This is used especially when it is *very* important that you do something.

> **I must** get my shoes mended.
> **I must** arrange an appointment.

Useful words

collect	to go and get someone or something from a place
a dry-cleaner's	a shop where clothes are cleaned with a special chemical rather than water
a camera	a piece of equipment for taking photographs or making films
repair	to fix something that has been damaged or is not working properly
an optician's	a shop where you can buy glasses and have your glasses repaired
a passport	an official document that you have to show when you enter or leave a country
mend	to repair something
arrange	to make plans for an event to happen

To say what you must not do, use **I mustn't ...** .

> **I mustn't** forget that my suit is at the dry-cleaner's.
> **You mustn't** miss your appointment.

Saying what you want to do

To say what you want to do, use **I'd like to ...** .

> **I'd like to** get these clothes washed.
> **I'd like to** transfer some money.
> **I'd like to** get to the optician's today.

If you are very eager to do something, use **I'd really like to ...** or **I'd love to ...** .

> **I'd really like to** spend the morning in town as I've got a few jobs to do.
> **I'd really like to** speak to someone who can advise me.
> **I'd really like to** get a hair appointment before my holiday.

> **I'd love to** have a cleaner.
> **I'd love to** have my hair cut at 'Stefano's' but it's so expensive.
> **I'd love to** get some new glasses.

Useful words

forget	to not remember something
miss	to not take part in a meeting or activity
transfer	to make something or someone go from one place to another
eager	wanting to do something very much
advise	to tell someone what you think they should do
a cleaner	a person whose job is to clean the rooms and furniture inside a building
expensive	costing a lot of money
glasses	two pieces of glass or plastic in a frame that some people wear in front of their eyes to help them to see

Asking for information

When you are asking for information you may need to get someone's attention before you can ask them a question. To do this, first say **excuse me**.

> **Excuse me**, where can I get my bag mended?
> **Excuse me**, is the pharmacy near here?

Use **Is ... ?** to ask general questions about things.

> **Is** the supermarket far from here?
> **Is** it far to the post office?

Use **Is there ... ?** or **Are there any ... ?** to ask whether something exists.

> Excuse me, **is there** a florist's near here?
> **Is there** an internet café in the area?
> **Is there** anyone who can help me?

> **Are there any** shops in this area?
> **Are there any** cafés near here?
> **Are there any** hairdressers nearby?

Useful words

a pharmacy	a place where you can buy medicines
a supermarket	a large shop that sells all kinds of food and other products for the home
a post office	a building where you can buy stamps and send post
a florist's	a shop where you can buy flowers
an Internet café	a café where there are computers which allow you to use the Internet
nearby	only a short distance away; close

To ask about the time that something will happen, use **What time ... ?** or **When ... ?**.

> **What time** does the shop shut?
> **What time** do I need to be here?

> **When** is the appointment?
> **When** shall I come back?

To ask about the price of something, use **How much ... ?**.

> **How much** is an eye test?
> **How much** are these glasses?
> **How much** do you charge to mend a pair of shoes?

To ask how much time something will take, use **How long ... ?**.

> **How long** is the appointment?
> **How long** do I have to wait to see someone?

To ask how to do something, use **How do you ... ?**.

> **How do you** open a bank account?
> **How do you** send money to the UK?

Useful words

shut	to close or be closed
an eye test	a test to find out how well you can see
charge	to ask someone to pay money for something
a pair	two things of the same size and shape that are used together
a bank account	an arrangement with a bank where they look after your money for you

Asking for things

To ask for something, use **Can I have ... ?** or **Could I have ... ?**. To be polite, use **please** at the beginning or end of the question.

> **Can I have** a receipt, **please**?
> **Can I have** a photocopy of the document, **please**?
> **Please can I have** a brochure?

> **Could I have** a leaflet, **please**?
> **Could I have** some information, **please**?
> **Could I have** a list of prices, **please**?

Another way of asking for a service is **I'd like ...** .

> **I'd like** some advice, please.
> **I'd like** an appointment next week, please.
> **I'd like** your opinion.

If it is important for you to have something, you can use **I need ...** .

> **I need** some help.
> **I need** some information.
> **You need** some form of identification.

Useful words

a receipt	a piece of paper that shows you have received goods or money from someone
a photocopy	a copy of a document that you make using a special machine
a document	an official piece of paper with important information on it
a brochure	a thin magazine with pictures that gives you information about a product or a service
a leaflet	a piece of paper containing information about a particular subject
a list	a set of names or other things that are written or printed one below the other
an opinion	what someone thinks about something
a form of	a type of
identification	a document that proves who you are

To ask if something that you want is available, use **Do you have ... ?**.

> **Do you have** a fax machine?
> **Do you have** any leaflets on the subject?
> **Do you have** those documents with you?
> **Do you have** your passport?

If you are asking someone if they can do something for you, use **Can you ... ?** or **Could you ... ?**. **Could you ... ?** is slightly more polite and formal than **Can you ... ?**. To be polite, use **please** at the beginning or end of these sentences.

> **Can you** give me a receipt, **please**?
> **Can you** call me on my mobile when it's fixed, **please**?
> **Can you** tell me how much it will cost?
> **Can you** tell me how much money I have in my account?

> **Could you** have a look at my camera?
> **Could you** check that these are the right documents?
> **Could you** send it to me by fax, **please**?
> **Could you** email the form to me, **please**?

Useful words

a fax machine	a special machine that is joined to a telephone line and that you use to send and receive documents
fix	to repair something
check	to make sure that something is correct
a fax	a special machine that is joined to a telephone line and that you use to send and receive documents
email	to send a written message from one computer to another
a form	a piece of paper with questions on it and spaces where you should write the answers

Making suggestions

If two or more people are trying to decide what to do or buy, use **We could ...** or **Shall we ... ?**.

> **We could** come back tomorrow.
> **We could** ask them what they would charge.
> **We could** show them your passport.

> **Shall we** try a different bank?
> **Shall we** come back later?
> **Shall we** ask for a refund?

To suggest what someone else can do or buy, use **You could ...** .

> **You could** contact your bank in the US.
> **You could** get the TV mended.
> **You could** use the launderette on Elm Street.

Use **How about ... ?** if you have an idea about what to do or buy.

> **How about** changing the appointment to Friday?
> **How about** asking to speak to the manager?
> **How about** changing your bank?

> **GOOD TO KNOW!**
> **How about + -ing**
> The verb that comes after **How about ... ?** must be in the -ing form.

Useful words

a refund	money that is returned to you because you have paid too much, or because you have returned goods to a shop
contact	to telephone someone or send them a message or a letter
a launderette	a place where people pay to use machines to wash and dry their clothes
a manager	a person who controls all or part of a business or organization

Talking about your plans

You will want to talk about things that you will do or buy that day, that week or that month. For plans that you are sure of, use **I'm going to ...** .

> **I'm going to** see if they can mend it.
> **I'm going to** pay by cheque.
> **We're going to** cancel the appointment.

To talk about something that you have just decided to do, use **I'll ...** .
> **I'll** ask at the bank.
> **I'll** change the appointment.
> **I'll** try to get a loan.

Use **Are you going to ... ?** or **Will you ... ?** to ask someone about their plans.

> **Are you going to** look around the apartment?
> **Are you going to** ask for a refund?
> **Are you going to** complain?

> **Will you** call the bank?
> **Will you** get the car washed while you're at the garage?
> **Will you** get your money back?

Useful words

a cheque	a printed piece of paper from a bank that you write an amount of money on and use to pay for something
cancel	to say that something that has been planned will not happen
a loan	an amount of money that you borrow
an apartment	a set of rooms for living in, usually on one floor and part of a larger building
complain	to say that you are not satisfied with someone or someone

● Listen out for

Here are some phrases you are likely to hear and use when asking for or using services.

Can I help you?
Can I help you at all?
It'll be ready tomorrow.
It's not ready yet.
We'll call you when it's ready.
It's ready for collection.
Do you have your receipt?
Do you need a receipt?
Do you have some form of identification?
Do you have your passport?
I'll need to see some form of identification.
What time of day would suit you best?
Do you have an appointment?
How would you like to pay?
I'll pay the full amount later.

Useful words
ready	prepared and able to be used
collection	when you go and get something or someone from a place
suit	to be convenient for you

🎧 **Listen to the conversation: Track 15**

Katie is speaking to her hairdresser.

A Hi, Katie, what can I do for you today?

B Well, I'd like a nice short haircut for the summer.

A Sure, what sort of style?

B I'd really like a haircut that I can wash and then leave to dry naturally.

A Right, do you have any pictures with you of the sort of style you'd like?

B No, I'm afraid not.

A Okay, shall we look in a hair magazine and get some ideas? What about this one?

B Oh, I'd love to have my hair cut like that but it really is *very* short!

A You could have this haircut but two or three centimetres longer. How would that be?

B That sounds great.

A How about changing the colour of your hair? Have you considered that?

B Oh, how much would that be?

A Prices for hair colouring start at around £20.

B No, I don't have that much money – I think I'll just have my hair cut.

A Sure – no problem.

🎧 **Listen to more phrases and practise saying them: Track 16**

Health

Get well soon!

If you become ill or have an accident, the phrases in this chapter will allow you to talk to a doctor, dentist or pharmacist. Use them to get the advice or treatment that you need.

Describing the problem

If you need to describe a medical problem, you can use **I've got ...** .

>**I've got** a temperature.
>**I've got** a cold.
>**I've got** asthma.

If you want to say which part of your body hurts, use **my ... hurts**.

>**My** back **hurts**.
>**His** foot **hurts**.
>**My** neck **hurts**.

If the pain you have is an ache, you can say which part of your body it is in by using **I've got ... ache**.

>**I've got** a head**ache**.
>**I've got** stomach **ache**.
>**She's got** tooth**ache**.

Useful words

temperature	when someone's body is too hot
a cold	an illness that makes liquid flow from your nose
asthma	an illness that makes it difficult to breathe
sore	painful and uncomfortable
your throat	the back of your mouth and inside your neck

You can talk about more general problems that you are having using **I feel ...** .

> **I feel** tired all the time.
> **I feel** sick.
> **I feel** better now.

Saying what happened

If you have an accident, you will need to explain what happened. You will need to use a past tense, such as **I fell ...** or **I burnt ...** .

> **I had** an accident.
> **I fell** down the stairs.
> **She burnt** her hand.
> **I hit** my head.

If your medical problem means that you cannot do something that you should be able to do, you can use **I can't ...** .

> **I can't** breathe properly.
> **I can't** move my fingers.
> **She can't** bend her arm.

If the accident is serious, and you have broken a bone in your body, use **I've broken ...** .

> I think **I've broken** my arm.
> **He's broken** his leg.
> **She's broken** a tooth.

Useful words

an accident	when something bad happens to a person by chance
stairs	a set of steps inside a building
burn	to injure a part of your body by fire
breathe	to take air into your lungs and let it out again
properly	in the correct way
bend	to change the position of a part of your body so that it is no longer straight

> **GOOD TO KNOW!**
> In English we say '**break my/his/her/your leg**', not 'break the leg'.

Asking for information

When you are asking for information you may need to get someone's attention before you can ask them a question. To do this, first say **excuse me**.

> **Excuse me**, is there a hospital nearby?
> **Excuse me**, how do I make an appointment?
> **Excuse me**, where is the X-ray department?

Use **Is there ... ?** to ask whether something exists near to where you are.

> **Is there** a dentist in the area?
> **Is there** a pharmacy on this street?
> **Is there** a doctor here?

When you need to get information about someone or something, start your questions with **What ... ?, Which ... ?, How ... ?, Who ... ?** or **When ... ?**.

> **What**'s this medicine for?
> **What** number do I call for an ambulance?
> **What**'s your doctor's address?
> **What** do I ask the pharmacist for?

Useful words

break a leg/ arm, etc.	to break the bone in a part of your body
an appointment	an arrangement to see someone at a particular time
an X-ray	a picture of the inside of someone's body
a dentist	a person whose job is to treat people's teeth
a pharmacy	a shop that sells medicines
an ambulance	a vehicle for taking people to hospital
a pharmacist	a person whose job is to prepare and sell medicines

Which doctor did you see last time?
Which street is the clinic in?
Which ward is she in?
Which is the best clinic?

How do I make an appointment?
How often do I take this medicine?
How long will he be in hospital?
How quickly can I see a doctor?

Who did you see last time?
Who is your doctor?
Who has come with you?
Who gave you this medicine?

When will my operation be?
When is the doctor coming?
When does visiting time start?
When do I have to take the tablets?

Use **What time ... ?** to ask about when things will happen.

What time is your appointment?
What time does the doctor's surgery open?
What time do I need to be at the hospital?

Useful words

a clinic	a place where people receive medical advice or treatment
a ward	a room in a hospital that has beds for many people
an operation	when a doctor cuts open a patient's body in order to remove, repair or replace a part
a surgery	the place where a doctor treats people

Many of the questions you will be asking can be answered by *yes* or *no*. The most common way of starting a question like this is with **Is ... ?**.

> **Is** it serious?
> **Is** the hospital far?
> **Is** the health centre open in the afternoon?

If you want to ask what to do about your problem, use **Should I ... ?**.

> **Should I** make another appointment?
> **Should I** stay in bed?
> **Should I** keep taking the tablets?

Asking for things

When you want to find out if something is available, use **Have you got ... ?**.

> **Have you got** anything for a headache?
> **Have you got** anything for hay fever?
> **Have you got** the doctor's phone number?

If you want to ask for something, start your sentence with **Can I have ... ?**.
To be polite, use **please** at the beginning or end of your sentence.

> **Can I have** an appointment for tomorrow, please?
> **Can I have** a packet of aspirins, please?
> Please **can I have** a plaster?

Useful words

a health centre	a place where people receive medical advice or treatment
a tablet	a small solid piece of medicine that you swallow
hay fever	an illness caused by plants that some people get in the summer
an aspirin	a medicine used to reduce pain and fever
a plaster	a small piece of sticky material used for covering small cuts on your body

Can I ... ? is also used in sentences where you are asking if you are allowed to do something or if something is possible.

> **Can I** see the dentist this morning?
> **Can I** talk to a nurse?
> **Can I** drive while I'm taking this medicine?
> When **can we** collect the results?

If you want to be very polite, you can use **Is it possible to ... ?**.

> **Is it possible to** see a different doctor?
> **Is it possible to** get an earlier appointment?
> **Is it possible to** meet the surgeon before my operation?

If you want to buy something in a pharmacy, use **Can I have ... ?** or **I'd like ...** .

> **I'd like** some cough medicine, please.
> **I'd like** a bandage.
> **I'd like** cream for dry skin.

If you are asking someone whether they can do something for you, you should use **Can you ... ?** or **Could you ... ?** . **Could you ... ?** is slightly more polite and formal than **Can you... ?** . To be polite, you can use **please** at the beginning or end of these sentences.

> **Can you** give me something for my earache, please?
> **Can you** send an ambulance straight away?
> **Can you** call a doctor, please?
> Please **can you** give me some advice on how to get fit?

Useful words

a surgeon	a doctor who is specially trained to do operations
a bandage	a long strip of cloth that is wrapped around an injured part of your body
cream	a type of medicine that you rub into your skin
earache	pain in your ear
fit	healthy and strong

Could you take us to the nearest hospital?
Could you check my blood pressure?
Could you put a bandage on this?
Could you lift your arm up for me?

Saying what you want to do

A simple and polite way of saying what you want to do is to use **I'd like to ...** .

I'd like to make an appointment with the doctor.
I'd like to see a dentist as soon as possible.
I'd like to talk to the pharmacist.
I'd like to speak to the doctor.

> **GOOD TO KNOW!**
> It is more polite to say **I'd like to** than simply 'I want to'.

Use **I'd prefer to ...** when you want to do one thing and not another.

I'd prefer to go to a local hospital.
I'd prefer to see a female doctor.
I'd prefer to have the operation next week.
I'd prefer not to take antibiotics.

You can talk about things that it is important for you to do or to have by using
I need ... .

I need some eyedrops.
He needs an operation on his leg.
You need to see a doctor.
I need to go to the pharmacy.

Useful words

antibiotics	medicine which cures infections by destroying harmful bacteria
local	in or relating to the area where you live
eyedrops	liquid medicine that you put in your eyes

Making suggestions

The most simple way to make a suggestion is to say **We could ...** or **You could ...** .

> **We could** ask the pharmacist.
> **We could** get some tissues at the pharmacy.
> **We could** phone his family.

> **You could** try that medicine I gave you.
> **You could** call this number for advice.
> **You could** try and get an appointment tomorrow.

If you want to suggest doing something with someone else, use **Shall we ... ?**.

> **Shall we** call a doctor?
> **Shall we** give him some medicine?
> **Shall we** try and eat more fresh fruit and vegetables?

How about ... ? is a slightly informal way of making suggestions of things to do or use.

> **How about** trying vitamin tablets?
> **How about** changing your diet a bit?
> **How about** walking to work instead of driving?

> **GOOD TO KNOW!**
> The verb that comes after **How about ... ?** must be in the -ing form.

Useful words

a tissue	a piece of thin, soft paper that you use to wipe your nose
your diet	the type of food that you regularly eat
instead of	in the place of someone or something

● Listen out for

Here are some useful phrases you are likely to hear or use at the doctor's or the hospital.

How are you?
What can I do for you?
How long have you been feeling like this?
Are you taking any other medicine?
Do you feel sick?
Where does it hurt?
The results are fine.
Are you allergic to antibiotics?
I'll give you a prescription.

My throat is very sore.
I've been feeling sick.
I've got a pain in my side.
I get out of breath very easily.
I'm not sleeping well.
I have no appetite.
I'm getting a lot of headaches.

Glossary

allergic	becoming ill when you eat, touch, or breathe something
a prescription	a piece of paper on which a doctor writes an order for medicine
out of breath	not able to breathe well
your appetite	the feeling that you want to eat

Philip is feeling ill and telephones the doctor's surgery to make an appointment.

A Good morning, doctor's surgery, how can I help you?

B Good morning, I'd like to make an appointment with the doctor.

A When would you like to come?

B Is today possible?

A No, today isn't possible, I'm afraid. But I can make you an appointment with the doctor for tomorrow morning, at... ten o'clock? Is that ok for you?

B Yes, that's fine. Thank you.

A Your name please?

B Philip Walsh.

A Philip Walsh. Great, so that's tomorrow at ten.

B Thank you, goodbye!

A Goodbye. See you tomorrow, Mr Walsh.

Philip is at the appointment with the doctor and they are discussing his symptoms.

A How can I help you?

B I've got a very sore throat and my head aches.

A Let me have a look. Can you open your mouth, please? Ah yes, the back of your throat is very swollen. How long has it been like this?

B About a week.

A Hmm, that's quite a long time. You need some antibiotics. Are you allergic to any antibiotics?

B No, I don't think so.

A OK then, I'll give you a prescription. Make sure you take all the tablets, even if you start to feel better.

🎧 **Listen to more phrases and practise saying them: Track 18**

Help!

Don't worry!

If you have a problem and you need help, use these phrases.

Describing the problem

If you are asking somebody for help, you will need to be able to describe the problem. Use **There is ...** to say what the problem is.

There's a smell of gas in my room.
There's water all over the floor.
There's a noise coming from the engine.
There are mice in the kitchen.

If the problem is that you do not have something you need, use **There isn't ...** .

There isn't any soap in the bathroom.
There isn't enough food for everyone.
There isn't any petrol in the car.
There aren't any towels in my room.

Useful words

gas	any substance that is not a liquid or a solid
an engine	the part of a car that produces the power to make it move
a mouse, *plural* mice	a small animal with a long tail
soap	a substance that you use with water for washing yourself
petrol	the fuel which you use in cars and some other vehicles to make the engine go
a towel	a piece of thick soft cloth that you use to dry yourself

For some problems, you can use **I've got ...** .

> **I've got** a problem.
> **I've got** a flat tyre.
> **She's got** heavy bags.
> **I've got** too much work.

If the problem is that you do not have something you need, use **I haven't got ...** .

> **I haven't got** her address.
> **She hasn't got** enough money.
> **He hasn't got** a car.
> **I haven't got** my phone with me.

If the problem is that you are not able to do something, use **I can't ...** .

> **I can't** drive.
> **I can't** turn the heating on.
> **We can't** open the bedroom door.
> **I can't** find my keys.

If you want to say that you do not understand something, use **I don't understand ...** .

> **I don't understand** what he's saying.
> **I don't understand** the instructions.
> **I don't understand** where we have to go.
> **I don't understand** how to use this phone.

Useful words

flat	with not enough air inside
a tyre	a thick round piece of rubber that fits around the wheels of cars and bicycles
heating	the equipment that is used for keeping a building warm
turn something on	to make a piece of equipment start working
instructions	things that people tell you to do

Saying what happened

You will probably need to explain to somebody what happened. You can use **I've ...** .

> **I've** forgotten my passport.
> **I've** had an accident.
> **We've** lost the key.
> **She's** broken her glasses.

Describing people and things

You can describe things that have been lost or stolen using **It's ...** .

> **It's** a black Honda with red seats.
> **It's** gold with three diamonds.
> **It's** a ladies' watch.
> **It's** a green suitcase with wheels.

When you are describing something, you may need to give more facts. Use **It's made of ...** to say what it is made of.

> **It's made of** leather.
> It's quite a small bag, and **it's made of** velvet.
> The beads are bright blue and **they're made of** glass.

Useful words

a passport	an official document that you have to show when you enter or leave a country
an accident	when something bad happens to a person by chance, sometimes causing injury or death
glasses	two pieces of glass or plastic in a frame, that some people wear in front of their eyes to help them to see better
a diamond	a hard clear stone that is very expensive and that is used for making jewellery
a suitcase	a case for carrying your clothes when you are travelling
leather	animal skin that is used for making shoes, clothes and bags
velvet	soft cloth that is thick on one side
a bead	a small piece of coloured glass, wood or plastic that is used for making jewellery

You may need to describe someone to the police, for example if they are lost or if you have seen them do something bad. Use **He's/She's ...** to say how old they are.

> **He's** five years old.
> **She's** eight.
> **She was** about thirty.
> **He was** about sixty.

Use **He's/She's got ...** to talk about what someone looks like.

> **She's got** short blond hair.
> **He's got** a beard.
> **She's got** a big nose.
> **They've** both **got** brown eyes.

To talk about someone's clothes, use **He's/She's wearing ...** .

> **She's wearing** jeans and a green T-shirt.
> **She's wearing** an orange blouse.
> **He's wearing** a black jacket.
> **They're wearing** long coats.

Useful words

blond	with pale-coloured hair
a beard	the hair that grows on a man's chin and cheeks
a blouse	a shirt for a girl or a woman
a swimming costume	a piece of clothing that is worn for swimming

Asking for information

You may need someone with a special skill to help you. Use **Is there ...** to ask about where to find them. You may need to get someone's attention before you can ask them a question. Use **Excuse me** to do this.

> Excuse me, **is there** a garage near here?
> **Is there** a police station near here?
> **Is there** anywhere I can hire a car in this town?
> **Is there** anyone who mends bikes here?

You may want to find out how to do something to help with your problem. Use **How ... ?** .

> **How** do I find his phone number?
> **How** can we find a plumber?
> **How** do I turn the computer on?
> **How** can she get help with her car?

If you want to know where to go to get help with your problem, use **Where ... ?** .

> **Where** is the nearest police station?
> **Where** is the lost property office?
> **Where** can he get his phone mended?
> **Where** can I buy a new battery?

Useful words

a garage	a place where you can have your car repaired
a police station	the local office of the police in a particular area
hire	to pay to use something
mend	to repair something
a plumber	a person whose job is to put in and repair things like water and gas pipes, toilets and baths
lost property	things that people have lost or accidentally left in a public place
a battery	a small object that provides electricity for things such as radios

Asking for things

If you want to ask for something that will help with your problem, use **Can I have ... ?**.

> **Can I have** the phone number of an electrician?
> **Can I have** another form, please?
> **Can I have** another blanket, please?

If you want to find out if something is available, use **Do you have ... ?**.

> **Do you have** a sewing kit?
> Excuse me, **do you have** a lost property office?
> Excuse me, **do you have** this document in English?

If you are asking someone whether they can do something for you, you should use **Can you ... ?** or **Could you ... ?**. **Could you ... ?** is slightly more polite and formal than **Can you ... ?**. To be polite, you can use **please** at the beginning or end of these sentences.

> **Can you** help me, please?
> **Can you** call the police?
> **Can you** mend my bike, please?

> **Could you** recommend an electrician?
> **Could you** show me how the shower works, please?
> **Could you** fix my laptop?

Useful words

an electrician	a person whose job is to repair electrical equipment
a form	a piece of paper with questions on it and spaces where you should write the answers
a sewing kit	the things you need to join pieces of cloth together
a document	an official piece of paper with important information on it
recommend	to suggest that someone would find a particular person or thing good or useful
a shower	a thing that you stand under, that covers you with water so you can wash yourself
a laptop	a small computer that you can carry with you

Saying what you want to do

To say what you want to do about your problem, use **I'd like to ...** .

> **I'd like to** make a complaint.
> **I'd like to** make a call.
> **I'd like to** speak to a police officer.

If you know that you do not want to do something, use **I don't want to ...** .

> **I don't want to** stay in this room.
> **I don't want to** leave my car here.
> **We don't want to** go to the hotel without our luggage.

Saying what you have to do

If it is important for you to do something, use **I have to ...** or **I need to ...** .

> **I have to** go to the British embassy.
> **I have to** leave my room by eleven.
> **I have to** tell my wife that we're safe.

> **I need to** speak to my lawyer.
> **I need to** make a call.
> **I need to** call an electrician.

Useful words

a complaint	when you say that you are not satisfied
a call	a telephone conversation
a police officer	a member of the police force
an embassy	the building where people who represent a foreign country work
a lawyer	a person whose job is to advise people about the law

Making suggestions

If two or more people are trying to decide what to do about a problem,
use **We could ...** or **Shall we ... ?**.

> **We could** go by train instead.
> **We could** ask my sister to help us.
> **We could** borrow some money.

> **Shall we** call the police?
> **Shall we** leave the car here?
> **Shall we** try and fix it ourselves?

To suggest what someone else can do about their problem, use **You could ...** .

> **You could** try switching it off and on again.
> **You could** try a different plug.
> **You could** ask for advice at reception.

Use **How about ... ?** if you have an idea about what to do about a problem.

> **How about** asking Mahmoud for help?
> **How about** taking it to the garage in the village?
> **How about** calling that electrician Marco knows?

Useful words

borrow	to use something that belongs to another person for a period of time and then return it
fix	to repair something
switch something off	to stop electrical equipment from working by operating a small control
switch something on	to make electrical equipment start working by operating a small control
a plug	a plastic object with metal pins that connects a piece of electrical equipment to the electricity supply
reception	the desk in a hotel or large building that you go to when you first arrive

---

> **GOOD TO KNOW!**
> **How about + -ing**
> The verb that comes after **How about ... ?** must be in the -ing form.

Talking about your plans

We often say **I'm going to ...** to talk about what we will do in the future.
Use **Are you going to ... ?** to ask someone about their plans.

> **I'm going to** phone the garage.
> **I'm going to** tell the police.
> **I'm going to** call for help on my mobile.
> **We're going to** phone an electrician.

> **Are you going to** fix the car today?
> **Are you going to** take it back to the shop?
> **Are you going to** complain?

Use **Will you ... ?** to ask if someone is going to do something.

> **Will you** call us when it's ready?
> **Will you** mend the cover at the same time?
> **Will you** charge us extra for this?

Useful words

a mobile	a telephone that you can carry wherever you go
complain	to say that you are not satisfied with someone or something
a cover	something that is put over an object to protect it
charge	to ask someone to pay money for something
extra	more than the normal amount

• Listen out for

Here are some key phrases you are likely to hear when you have some kind of problem.

What's the problem?
What happened?
Is there anything I can do to help?
Can I have your insurance details?
What's been taken?
Can I have your address, please?
Can I have your driving licence?
Were there any witnesses?
Please fill in this form.

Can you help me?
I need some help.
I have a problem that I need help with.
There's been an accident.
My car's broken down.
The shower/phone/radio doesn't work.
Could you mend my watch/shoes/bag?
Could you change the tyre/oil?

Useful words

insurance	an agreement that you make with a company in which you pay money to them regularly, and they pay you if something bad happens to you or your property
details	the facts about something
a driving licence	a document that shows that you have passed a driving test and that you are allowed to drive
a witness	a person who saw an event such as an accident or a crime
break down	to stop working

🎧 Listen to the conversation: Track 19

Katie's bag has been stolen. She's phoning her father for help.

A Hi Dad. I've got a problem – I'm in a café and someone's stolen my bag. I don't know what to do.

B Oh... Have you told the police?

A No, I wasn't sure if I should.

B You could ask the café owners to call them.

A OK, I'll do that. It's terrible – I've lost my money, my keys – everything! And I'm worried the people in the café won't believe me. Could you come over and help me?

B I'm really sorry, Katie – I have to be in a meeting in ten minutes. How about calling your Mum?

A OK, I'll call her. Thanks, Dad.

Scott has missed his train, and he needs to get to an important meeting. He is talking to his colleague Laura.

A Hi, Laura, I need some help.

B Sure, what's the problem?

A I've missed my train, and I need to be in Milan by 5 o'clock this afternoon.

B How about flying? There's an airport in Milan.

A Could you check the times for me? I'm not on the Internet here.

B Are you coming back tomorrow?

A No, I'm going to meet Andrea on Thursday.

B OK, there's a flight at 12 – you need to get to the airport an hour before.

A How do I get to the airport from here?

B It's probably best to get a taxi.

A OK, thanks for your help, Laura.

 Listen to more phrases and practise saying them: Track 20

Telephoning and writing

Getting in touch

The phrases in this unit will help you communicate with people by phone, letter, email or text.

Making a telephone call

If you want to tell someone that you need to make a phone call, use **I need to ...** .

> **I need to** make a call
> **I need to** phone my wife.
> **I need to** call my brother.

To ask for a phone number, use **Do you have ... ?**.

> **Do you have** Mrs Kay's number, please?
> **Do you have** the number of a taxi firm?
> **Do you have** a mobile number?

You can also ask questions using **What ... ?** .

> **What's** her phone number?
> **What's** the code for the United States?
> **What** number do I have to dial for room service?

Useful words

a mobile	a telephone that you can carry wherever you go
a code	a group of numbers or letters that give information about something
dial	to press the buttons on a telephone in order to call someone
room service	when meals are brought to your room in a hotel

When the person you're calling answers

Once you've made the call and someone answers, you will need to tell them who you are. Use **Hello, it's ... (here)** .

> **Hello**, **it's** Marta Fuentes **here**.
> **Hello** Mr Hall, **it's** Alex Ronaldson **here**.
> **Hello**, is Stéphanie in? **It's** Marie.

To explain more about who you are, use **I'm ...** .

> **I'm** a colleague of Su's.
> **I'm** a friend of Oleg's.
> **I'm** Mr Cadey's daughter.

To check that you are speaking to the right person, use **Is that ... ?** .

> **Is that** Amandeep?
> **Is that** Dr Gardner?
> **Is that** the police station?

If you want to ask for somebody, use **Is ... there?** or **Can I speak to ... ?**.

> **Is** Olivier **there**, please?
> **Is** your Dad **there**?
> **Is** Mrs Rawle **there**, please?

> **Can I speak to** Rebecca, please?
> **Can I speak to** one of your parents?
> **Can I speak to** someone in the sales department?

Useful words
a colleague   a person someone works with
a department   one of the sections in an organisation

> **GOOD TO KNOW!**
> If the person you want to speak to is not there, you may hear
> **Sorry, he's not here.** or **Sorry, she's not in.** If the person is there,
> you may hear **Who's calling, please?** . If you hear this, you should
> say your name.

We often start a telephone conversation, especially with someone we know,
by asking about their health, using **How are you?** .

> Hello, Otto. **How are you?**
> Hi, it's Chuck. **How are you?**

> **GOOD TO KNOW!**
> To answer that question, use **I'm fine, thanks.** or **I'm good, thanks.** .
> If you are not well, you could say **Not great, really.** or **Not too good,**
> **actually.** .

Saying why you're calling

To say why you are calling, use **I'm phoning/calling/ringing about ...** or
I'm phoning/calling/ringing to ... .

> **I'm phoning about** tomorrow night.
> **I'm calling about** your ad in the paper.
> **I'm ringing about** the job.

> **I'm phoning to** talk to Marie.
> **I'm calling to** find out whether you can repair our gas boiler.
> **I'm ringing to** get some information about holidays in Spain.

Useful words

an ad	information that tells you about something such as a product, an event, or a job
repair	to fix something that has been damaged or is not working properly
a boiler	a piece of equipment that provides hot water for a house

To explain where you are or what company or organisation you are from, use **I'm calling from ...** .

> **I'm calling from** work.
> **I'm calling from** the doctor's surgery.
> **I'm calling from** Mr Brigham's office.

If you want to ask whether you can do something, use **Can I ... ?** .

> **Can I** leave a message?
> **Can I** call back later?
> **Can I** give you my mobile number?

To ask someone else to do something, use **Could you ... ?** .

> **Could you** ask her to call me, please?
> **Could you** put me through to Johanna, please?
> **Could you** give her a message?

Giving information

When you make a phone call, you may be asked to give your own phone number. Use **My (phone) number is ...** .

> **My** home **phone number is ...**
> ... and **my** mobile **number is ...**
> **My** hotel **phone number** is ...

Useful words

a surgery	a building where doctors treat people
a message	a piece of information that you send to someone
call (someone) back	to telephone someone in return for a call they made to you
put someone through	to connect someone to someone else on the telephone

> **GOOD TO KNOW!**
> In English, we usually say the numbers in a telephone number separately, not as 'twenty five/forty three' etc. When there are two numbers the same next to each other, we say **double**. The number o is usually said like the letter 'O'. So the number 0223 would be said as 'O double two three'.

To give details of where you can be contacted, use **You can contact me on ...** .

You can contact me on 0998 02 46 23.
You can contact me on my mobile.
You can contact me on my sister's number.

Answering the telephone

It is very common to say **Hello?** when we answer the phone. At work, people sometimes answer by saying their name.

If the person who is calling asks for you, say **Speaking.** .

'Can I speak to Lily, please?' '**Speaking.**'
'Is Ms Rathbone there, please?' 'Yes, **speaking.**'

To ask what the person calling wants to do, use **Would you like ... ?** .

Would you like to leave a message?
Would you like him to call you back?
Would you like to call back a bit later?

Ending a telephone call

When you end a telephone call, say **Goodbye.** in the same way as you would if you were leaving someone. This is often shortened to **Bye.** .

> Thanks for your help. **Goodbye**.
> OK then, **goodbye**.

> Right, **bye** Raymond! Talk to you later!
> **Bye**, darling. See you soon.

When you say goodbye, you may want to send your best wishes to someone else. In an informal situation use **Say hello to ...** , and in a more formal situation use **Give ... my best wishes.** .

> **Say hello to** your family.
> **Say hello to** your sister for me.

> **Give** your father **my best wishes**.
> **Give** Ning **my best wishes**.

● Listen out for

Here are some useful phrases you may hear when using the telephone.

Who's calling, please?
Please hold the line.
Hang on a minute, I'll get him.
You've got the wrong number.
Do you have the extension number?
His line is engaged.
I'll put you through.
Please leave a message after the tone.
This call will cost 10 pence per minute.
Please call back later.
Thanks for calling.

Useful words

hold the line	to wait on the telephone
extension number	the number of a telephone that is connected to a main telephone in an organisation
engaged	already being used
put someone through	to connect you to someone else on the telephone

Writing letters and emails

Here are some useful phrases for writing letters and emails.

Dear Paul, ...
Hi Marta!

Love, Naïma.
Lots of love, Charlotte.

All the best, Maciej.
Cheers, Lucien.

Regards, Clive.
Kind regards, Bella.
Yours, Sujata.

To: nadia@ntlworld.com

Cc:

Subject: Tomorrow evening

Hi Clara!
Do you want to go to the cinema tomorrow evening? Penelope Cruz's new film is on at 8.30.

If not, how about lunch on Saturday?

See you soon, I hope

love,
Nadia, x

GOOD TO KNOW!
When you say your email address, say 'at' for @ and 'dot' for .
So this address is: nadia at ntlworld dot com.

157 North St
Newtown
NT4 8QT

Your own address

14th February, 2015 — *The date*

Dear Isabella

Thanks very much for your last letter – it was great to hear from you and to hear all your news. You seem to be having a great time in China!

Thanks also for the photographs. China looks amazing, and it was good to see you looking so well and so happy.

There's not much happening here. I'm working hard for my exams. I need to pass them all to do the journalism course I want to do next year. English and History should be OK, but I'm worried about maths – it's so difficult!

Your Mum said you may be coming home for a week or two in August. If you are, let me know the dates and we can arrange to meet up.

Hope to see you then!

Martina, x

GOOD TO KNOW!
Sometimes people use an 'x' at the end of an email or a letter. You should only use 'x' with people you know very well, as it represents a kiss.

Mr Andrew Kennedy
37 Church Rd
Glasgow
G64 3PH
UK

The postcode
comes after
the name of
the town.

Starting a formal letter or email

Dear Mr Provence, ...
Dear Madam, ...
Dear Sir or Madam, ...

Ending a formal letter or email

Yours faithfully, Anton Smit
Yours sincerely, Ali Sharpe

GOOD TO KNOW!
We use **Yours sincerely** to end a letter where we have used
the person's name, and **Yours faithfully** where we did not use
the name, but something like 'Dear Sir/Madam'.

Ending a formal letter or email in a slightly more friendly way

Best wishes, Valentina Clark
Kind regards, Tony Bishop

37 Church St
Glasgow
G64 3PH

Your own
address

The Manager
Munchies Restaurant
39 High St
Bridgetown
BD78 8AL

Name and
address of
the person/
company you
are writing to

2 June 2014

The date

Dear Sir/Madam,

I am writing to complain about a meal we had in your restaurant last Wednesday.

I had booked a table for four, for my wife's birthday, but when we arrived there were no free tables, and we had to wait more than half an hour to sit down.

My wife's steak was burnt, and the waiter was very rude when we told him this. From a menu of 8 desserts, only two were available, and their quality was very poor.

I feel that we were treated very badly, and would like to receive a refund of at least half the bill.

Yours faithfully,

Colin Wilson

Colin Wilson

Texting

Texting is a very popular and quick way to communicate. We often use special abbreviations for texting. Here are some common ones. Some people write them using capital letters.

@	at		lo	hello
2	to or two		lol	laughing out loud
2day	today		m8	mate
2moro	tomorrow		pls	please
4	for		pov	point of view
aml	all my love		r	are
asap	as soon as possible		rofl	rolling on the floor laughing
atm	at the moment		some1	someone
b4	before		soz/sry	sorry
btw	by the way		spk	speak
c	see		syl	see you later
cm	call me		tx/thx	thanks
cu	see you		u	you
cul	see you later		ur	your/you're
fyi	for your information		w8	wait
gr8	great		wan2	want to
ic	I see		wk	week
im(h)o	in my (humble) opinion		wrk	work
l8	late		xlnt	excellent
l8r	later		y	why

> 🎧 **Listen to the conversation: Track 21**

Katie is trying to phone her friend Saskia, but Saskia's father answers the phone.

A Hello?

B Oh... Mr Greene. It's Katie here. Can I speak to Saskia, please?

A She's not here at the moment.

B Oh... I'm ringing about the play we're going to tomorrow evening.

A Would you like to call back later?

B That's a bit difficult because I'm going out now. Could you give her a message, please?

A Sure.

B Could you tell her to meet me at the theatre at 7 o'clock tomorrow evening. If she can't, she should leave a message on my mobile or text me.

A Fine, Katie, I'll tell her.

B Thanks, Mr Greene.

B That's OK. Nice to hear from you.

Rudi has seen an advert for a job he is interested in. He phones the number.

A Hello, could I speak to Mr Jenkins, please?

B Speaking.

A My name's Rudi Thorne, and I'm ringing about the job in your café.

B Oh yes? Have you worked in a café before?

A Yes, my uncle has a café in Perth and I've worked for him in the holidays.

B That's good. Would you be able to come in for an interview?

A Yes, when shall I come?

B I'm not sure yet because my colleague Doug Young wants to be at the interviews too. Can I call you back later?

A Of course. I'll give you my number.

🎧 **Listen to more phrases and practise saying them: Track 22**

Work

At work

Most types of work involve a lot of speaking. You have to arrange to meet people and you have to speak to people who are buying things from you. There are many different things that you need to be able to say at work. The phrases in this unit will help you in all these different work situations.

Greetings

Use **Hello ...** as a general greeting. It is polite to say **hello** to anyone in any work situation.

> **Hello** Anton.
> **Hello** Dr Sasaki.

Use **Good morning, Good afternoon** or **Good evening** in slightly more formal work situations, for example if you are giving a talk to a large group of people.

> **Good morning** Carina.
> **Good afternoon** everyone. I'd like to start by thanking you all for coming here.

> **GOOD TO KNOW!**
> In English, there is no greeting starting with 'Good' that is used for the whole day.

Often, when you are at work, you meet people that you do not know. You need to know how to greet these people. To tell someone your name, use **Hello, I'm ...** .

> **Hello**, **I'm** Carlos Sanchez.
> **Hello**, **I'm** Lanying Peng.

If a person tells you their name, reply by saying **Pleased to meet you**. Then tell them your name by first saying **I'm ...** .

> **Pleased to meet you**. I'm Carole Durand.
> **Pleased to meet you**. I'm Curt Haussman.

You may also want to tell the person what your job is in the company that you work for. To do this, say **I'm ...** .

> **I'm** the marketing manager for the UK.
> **I'm** the head of sales for Western Europe.

Use **Goodbye ...** when you leave someone at work.

> **Goodbye** Frida.

See you ... is a slightly informal way of saying goodbye to someone at work that you know you will see again.

> **See you** later.
> **See you** tomorrow.
> **See you** on Thursday.

Introducing people

You may want to introduce a new person to a colleague. To do this, use **this is ...** saying their full name after.

> Leila, **this is** Chen Wang.
> Marco, **this is** Yuko Miyuki.
> Charlotte, **this is** Anna-Maria Delgado. Anna-Maria, **this is** Charlotte Walker.

Useful words

marketing	the work of advertising and selling a product
a manager	a person who controls all or part of a business or organization
a head	the person who is in charge of a business or organization
sales	the part of a company that sells its products or services
later	at a time in the future
tomorrow	the day after today
introduce	to tell people each other's names so that they can get to know each other
a colleague	a person that someone works with

Talking about your plans

When you are with your colleagues, you will want to talk about things that you will do that day, that week or that month. For plans that you are sure of, use **I'm going to ...** .

> **I'm going to** email Faisal this morning.
> **I'm going to** call the Spanish office today.
> **We're going to** meet Channa to talk about book sales.

To talk about your plans, you can also use **I plan to ...** .

> **I plan to** finish the work next month.
> **I plan to** visit the Italian office in June.
> **I plan to** travel later this year.

You can also use **I intend to ...** .

> **I intend to** ask him that question when we meet.
> **I intend to** work on the report this Friday.
> **I intend to** invite her to the meeting.

To talk about a plan that you are not totally sure about, you can use **I hope to ...** .

> **I hope to** write the report this week.
> **I hope to** meet with Francine while I'm in Amsterdam.
> **We hope to** finish the project by December 12th.
> **They hope to** come to the meeting in June.

Useful words

email	to send a written message from one computer to another
an office	a place where people work sitting at a desk, or the people in that place
sales	the number of things that a company sells
a report	a piece of writing that gives information about a subject
invite	to ask someone to come to an event
a meeting	an event at which a group of people come together to discuss things or make decisions
a project	a plan that takes a lot of time and effort

Use **Are you going to ... ?** or **Will you ... ?** to ask someone about their plans.

> **Are you going to** ask Guy to come to the meeting?
> **Are you going to** email the sales team too?
> **Are you going to** meet Per while you're in Stockholm?
> **Is he going to** tell you when he has finished the work?

> **Will you** finish the work on time?
> **Will you** be at the meeting tomorrow?
> **Will you** ask Rohit to comment on the report?
> **Will he** give us the information?

Making suggestions

To say to a colleague that you will do something, use **I can ...** .

> **I can** invite Yuko to the meeting.
> **I can** check these figures.
> **I can** speak to Svetlana, if you like.

You can also use **I'll ...** to offer to do something.

> **I'll** write an introduction.
> **I'll** order another computer.
> **I'll** email Santiago, if you like.

> **GOOD TO KNOW!**
> When people use **I can ...** or **I'll ...** to say they will do something,
> they often add **if you like** at the end of the sentence.

Useful words

a team	any group of people who work together
comment	to give your opinion or say something about something
check	to make sure that something is correct
figures	amounts or prices expressed as numbers
an introduction	the part at the beginning of a piece of writing that tells you what the piece of writing is about
order	to ask for something to be sent to you from a company

To suggest something that you and your colleagues could do, use **We could ...** .

> **We could** give the work to someone else.
> **We could** ask Diana for advice.
> **We could** refuse to pay them.

Another way to suggest something that you and your colleagues could do is **Shall we ... ?**.

> **Shall we** finish now?
> **Shall we** change the date of the meeting?
> **Shall we** discuss this with Piotrek?

Saying what you have to do

To tell your colleagues that it is very important that you do something, use **I have to ...** .

> **I have to** finish this before I leave.
> **I have to** email Cyrus and tell him.
> **You have to** call the customer when it's ready.

To say what you have to do in a strong way, you can also use **I must ...** .

> **I must** call Sergei this morning.
> **I must** finish this report today.
> **You must** write down the customer's telephone number.

Useful words

advice	what you say to someone when you are telling them what you think they should do
refuse	to say that you will not do something
a date	a particular day and month or a particular year
discuss	to talk about something
a customer	someone who buys something from a shop or website

When you want to say that you should or ought to do something, use **I should ...** .

> **I should** email Henrik as well.
> **I should** offer the work to Sam.
> **I should** let them know I don't want the job so they can offer it to someone else.

To ask what someone has to do, use **Do you have to ... ?**.

> **Do you have to** tell your boss?
> **Do you have to** give them an answer now?
> **Do you have to** be in the office tomorrow?

Asking for information

The simplest way of asking if something is a particular thing is **Is it ... ?**.

> **Is it** quick?
> **Is it** easy to use?
> **Is it** expensive?

To ask whether there is something, use **Is there ... ?**.

> **Is there** a printer?
> **Is there** a coffee machine here?
> **Are there** any spare chairs we could use?

Useful words

a job	the work that someone does to earn money
offer	to ask someone if they would like to have something
a boss	the person in charge of you at the place where you work
expensive	costing a lot of money
a printer	a machine for printing copies of computer documents on paper

To ask for information about something, use **What ... ?**.

> **What**'s her name?
> **What**'s his email address?
> **What** do you think?

To ask about the place that something or someone is, use **Where ... ?**.

> **Where** is Peder?
> **Where** is the fax machine?
> **Where** did Ali go?

To ask about the time that something will happen, use **When ... ?**.

> **When** can we meet?
> **When** does she start work?
> **When** does Mira usually leave the office?

Asking for things

To ask a colleague if you can have something, use **Can I ... ?**.

> **Can I** use your phone, please?
> **Can I** have her telephone number?
> **Can I** see those figures, please?

A more polite way to ask a colleague if you can have something is **Could I ... ?**.

> **Could I** borrow this book, please?
> **Could I** use your computer?
> **Could I** sit here for a moment, please?

Useful words

a fax machine   a machine that is joined to a telephone line and that allows you to send and receive documents

borrow   to use something that belongs to someone else for a period of time and then return it

To ask a colleague if they can do something for you, use **Can you ... ?**.

> **Can you** help me with the printer, please?
> **Can you** pass me those papers, please?
> **Can you** check these figures, please?

A more polite way to ask a colleague if they can do something for you is
Could you ... ?.

> **Could you** send me that report, please?
> **Could you** speak to Jingfei about the problem?
> **Could you** close that door, please?

GOOD TO KNOW!
When people are asking for something using **Can I/Could I ... ?** or
Can you/Could you ... ?. they often add **please** at the end of the
sentence to be polite.

Apologizing

Sometimes when we are at work, there are problems and we make mistakes.
When this happens we may need to say we are sorry to a colleague or
a customer. To apologize, use **I'm sorry ...** or **Sorry ...** .

> **I'm sorry** – I've forgotten your name.
> **I'm sorry**, I've forgotten to bring those figures with me.
> **I'm sorry** I'm late.

> **Sorry** – I have to leave now.
> **Sorry**, I didn't hear what you were saying.
> **Sorry**, I didn't introduce you.

Useful words

pass	to give an object to someone
apologize	to say that you are sorry
forget	to not remember something
late	after the time that something should start or happen

If you have to tell a colleague or a customer that there is a problem or that something bad has happened, start your sentence with **I'm afraid ...** .

> **I'm afraid** I'm going to be late.
> **I'm afraid** I can't come to the meeting.
> **I'm afraid** there's a problem with your order.
> **I'm afraid** the meeting has been cancelled.

GOOD TO KNOW!

If someone apologizes to you, reply **That's all right.** or **Don't worry.** This lets the person who is apologizing know that you are not angry with them or that the problem is not important.

Expressing opinions

If you want to give your opinion about something, use **I think ...** .

> **I think** these meetings are very useful.
> **I think** we should start now.
> **I think** you're right.

You can also give your opinion of something by saying **In my opinion ...** .

> **In my opinion**, it is too expensive.
> **In my opinion**, we should give the job to Holga Erikson.
> **In my opinion**, she's the wrong person for the job.

Useful words

an order	the thing that someone has asked for
cancel	to say that something that has been planned will not happen
an opinion	what someone thinks about something
useful	helpful for doing something
right	correct

To ask someone for their opinion, say **What do you think of ... ?** .

> **What do you think of** their products?
> **What do you think of** Helga's report?
> **What do you think of** these meetings?

You can also ask someone for their opinion by saying **What's your opinion of ... ?**.

> **What's your opinion of** the new manager?
> **What's your opinion of** Jonas?

Agreeing and disagreeing

If you think that what someone has said is right, say **I agree ...** .

> **I agree**. I think it's very successful.
> **I agree** with Henk.
> Yes, **I agree** with you.

You can also agree with what someone has said by saying **You're right**.

> **You're right**. Sales have to increase.
> **You're right**. We've improved a lot over the years.
> I think **you're right**. She's a very good manager.

Useful words

a product	something that you make or grow in order to sell
successful	doing or getting what you wanted
increase	to get bigger in some way
improve	to get better

If you think that what someone has said is wrong, say **I disagree ...** .

> **I disagree**. I think she's very good at her job.
> **I disagree** with you here.
> I'm afraid **I disagree**.

GOOD TO KNOW!

When people say **I disagree**, they often start the sentence with **I'm afraid**. This sounds more polite and less forceful.

● Listen out for

Here are some important phrases you are likely to hear and use at work.

Can I speak to Taylor Jackson, please?
Can I say who is calling, please?
I'm afraid she's not at her desk.
Can I take a message?
Will you be at the meeting?
Is everyone here?
Have you met Charles?
Thanks for all your work on this.
Thanks for finishing this so quickly.
I don't think these figures are accurate.
I've checked the figures.
The report contains some mistakes.
Have you read the report?
I need to check my email.
I got an email from him this morning.
She sent me an email yesterday.
I'll need to speak to my manager.

Useful words

a desk	a table that you sit at to write or work
a message	a piece of information that you send to someone
accurate	correct
a mistake	something that is not correct

🎧 Listen to the conversation: Track 23

Two people who work for the same company meet for the first time at a sales conference.

A Hello, I'm Yasmin Peters.

B Pleased to meet you. I'm Jamie Harker.

A Do you work in sales too?

B Yes, I'm the sales manager for Eastern Europe.

A Right. Could I sit here for a moment? I've been standing all day!

B Of course – take a seat. What did you think of the talk today?

A I thought it was really good.

B I agree. Claudia Churchill is a really good speaker.

A You're right – she's excellent.

B I'm afraid I have to leave now. I have to catch a train to the airport and I don't know how often the trains go.

A That's all right. I can look up train times on my mobile if you like.

B Could you? That would be great.

A What time is your flight?

B Eight o'clock but I have to be at the airport an hour before.

A Okay. So if you leave now, there's a train in fifteen minutes.

B That sounds perfect. It was nice meeting you, Yasmin.

A You too, Jamie. See you again in December at the winter sales conference!

🎧 Listen to more phrases and practise saying them: Track 24

studying

In the classroom

If you are at school, college, or university, the phrases in this section will allow you to talk about your studies. You will be able to use them in class, as well as for finding information you need and expressing your own opinions about the subjects you are studying.

Asking for information

When you need to get information about something, start your questions with **What ... ?**, **Which ... ?**, **Who ... ?**, **Where ... ?** or **When ... ?**.

> **What**'s this book about?
> **What** does the word 'fluent' mean?

> **Which** room is the maths lesson in?
> **Which** computer shall I use?

> **Who** teaches you for chemistry?
> **Who** should I give the money for the school trip to?

> **Where** are the new textbooks?
> **Where** is my school bag?

> **When** is the lunch break?
> **When** is your next lesson?

Useful words

fluent	able to speak a particular language easily and correctly
chemistry	the science of the structure of gases, liquids and solids, and how they change
a trip	a journey that you make to a particular place and back again
a textbook	a book that is used by people studying a particular subject
your lunch break	a time in the middle of the day when you stop work to eat a meal

A very common way of asking how to do something is to use the phrase
How do you ... ?.

> **How do you** spell that?
> **How do you** divide a small number by a bigger number?
> **How do you** turn this computer on?

Use **Is there ... ?** or **Are there any ... ?** to ask whether something exists.
You use these phrases especially when you want to have something to use.

> **Is there** any paper left?
> **Is there** a spare laptop in here?
> **Are there** any pens in that box?
> **Are there** any more calculators?

If you want to ask your teacher for some advice about what to do, use **Should
I ... ?**.

> **Should I** write on both sides of the paper?
> **Should I** put labels on the diagram?
> **Should I** use a dictionary for this work?

Useful words

divide	to find out how many times one number can fit into another number
spare	not being used by anyone else
a laptop	a small computer that you can carry with you
a calculator	a small electronic machine that you use to calculate numbers
a label	a word or phrase written on something to show what it is
a diagram	a simple drawing used to explain something
a dictionary	a book in which the words and phrases of a language are listed, together with their meanings

Expressing opinions

You may be asked to express an opinion about what you are studying.
Use **I think ...** .

> **I think** the answer is 354.
> **I think** the best book on the subject is Antonia Fraser's 'The Six Wives of Henry VIII'.
> **I think** the poet is expressing his fear of death.
> **I think** we should try the experiment again.

To say that you do not think something is true, use **I don't think ...** .

> **I don't think** this translation is very good.
> **I don't think** the information on this website is very reliable.
> **I don't think** the author wanted the book to be political.
> **I don't think** the library has that book.

To ask for someone's opinion about the quality of something, use **What do you think of ... ?** .

> **What do you think of** Mr Cowell's lessons?
> **What do you think of** the science labs here?
> **What do you think of** the sports facilities?

Useful words	
a poet	a person who writes poems (= pieces of writing in which the words are chosen for their beauty and sound, and arranged in short lines)
express	to show what you think or feel
an experiment	a scientific test that you do in order to discover what happens to something
a translation	a piece of writing or speech that has been put into a different language
reliable	probably correct
a library	a place where books, newspapers, DVDs and music are kept for people to use and borrow
a lab	a building or a room where scientific work is done
facilities	something such as rooms, buildings or pieces of equipment that are used for a particular purpose

To agree with someone's opinion, use **I agree.** or **You're right.**. If you want to say who you agree with, use **with**.

> 'Miss Grandison is a great teacher.' **I agree**. I love her lessons.'
> **I agree** that Ghandi was a great man.
> **I agree with** Mette – it's best to take a break from studying now and then.

> 'I think this chemical must be sulphur.' **You're right.'**
> I think **you're right**.
> **Gerd is right** – The French Revolution began in 1789.

If you do not agree with someone, you can use **I don't think so.** .

> 'It's good to listen to music while you study.' **I don't think so.'**
> 'This homework is easy.' **I don't think so**. Can you help me with it?'
> 'Economics is really interesting.' **I don't think so**. I find the lessons quite boring.'

Asking for and giving explanations

You will often need to ask your teacher to explain things. The simplest way is to use **Why ... ?** .

> **Why** do I need to heat the liquid?
> **Why** are there no women poets on this list?
> **Why** can't fish breathe out of water?

Useful words

a break	a short period of time when you have a rest
sulphur	a yellow chemical that has an unpleasant smell
a revolution	an attempt by a group of people to change their country's government by using force
economics	the study of the way that money and industry are organised in a society

Could you explain ... ? can be used to ask your teacher to explain something. Your teacher might use it to ask you to explain something too.

> **Could you explain** why the flame changes colour?
> **Could you explain** what happens when the cell divides?
> **Could you explain** how to do this calculation?

To ask for a reason, use **What is the reason ... ?** .

> **What is the reason** that birds fly south in winter?
> **What is the reason** for the change in temperature?
> **What is the reason** for Juliet's happiness?

To give an explanation, use **Because ...** .

> **Because** he was working in Paris at that time.
> Your answer was not correct **because** you put the decimal point in the wrong place.
> **Because** he was not able to write any more.

GOOD TO KNOW!
In speech, it is fine to use **because** at the beginning of a sentence, although it is not good to do this in writing.

Useful words

a flame	the bright burning gas that comes from a fire
a cell	the smallest part of an animal or plant
divide	to separate into smaller parts
a calculation	when you find out a number or amount by using mathematics
a decimal point	the dot that you use when you write a number as a decimal

Explaining a problem

To explain a general problem, use **I've got a problem ...** . Use the preposition **with** to talk about a thing that is causing your problem.

> **I've got a problem** – I want to do French and history, but the classes are at the same time.
> **I've got a problem** – this homework has to be done by tomorrow, but I haven't got the books I need.
> **I've got a problem with** my essay – it's too long and I don't know what to cut out.
> **I've got a problem with** my laptop.

If you need something for your studies but you haven't got it, use **I haven't got ...** .

> **I haven't got** the books I need.
> **I haven't got** Internet access at the moment.
> **I haven't got** enough time to finish my essay.

If you are not able to do something, use **I can't ...** .

> **I can't** see the screen.
> **I can't** read his writing.
> **I can't** remember what we have to do for the next biology class.
> **I can't** find my notes.

Useful words

history	the study of events that happened in the past
an essay	a short piece of writing on a subject
cut something out	to remove something
access	when you are able or allowed to see or use information or equipment
a screen	a flat surface on a piece of electronic equipment, such as a television or a computer, where you see pictures or words
biology	the scientific study of living things
a note	something that you write down to remind yourself of something

Saying what you have to do

To tell people what you have to do, use **I have to ...** or **I need to ...** .

> **I have to** get to my chemistry lesson.
> **I have to** finish this essay by Monday.
> **I have to** prepare for my exam.
>
> **I need to** read this book.
> **I need to** buy a good dictionary.
> **I need to** ask the teacher to help me.

If something is important, you could use **It is important for me to ...** .

> **It is important for me to** pass this exam.
> **It is important for me to** find my notes.
> **It is important for me to** work as hard as possible.

Asking for permission

To ask your teacher if you can do something, use **Can I ... ?** .

> **Can I** use the computer?
> **Can I** have a bit longer to do this homework?
> **Can I** use a dictionary?
> **Can I** borrow this book until next week?

Useful words

prepare	to get ready for something
borrow	to use something that belongs to another person for a period of time and then return it

To ask if your teacher is happy for you to do something, use **Is is OK ... ?** or **Do you mind if ... ?** .

> **Is it OK** to use a calculator?
> **Is it OK** to write in the margin?
> **Is it OK** if we work together?

> **Do you mind if** my essay's a bit longer than you said?
> **Do you mind if** we take some chairs from your classroom?
> **Do you mind if** we look on the Internet?

You could also see if something is allowed by using **Are we allowed to ... ?** .

> **Are we allowed to** use dictionaries?
> **Are we allowed to** work in pairs?
> **Are we allowed to** discuss the answers?

Asking for things

To ask for something, use **Can I have ... ?** or **Could I have ... ?**. To be polite, use **please** at the beginning or end of the question.

> **Can I have** a handout, please?
> **Can I have** a ruler?
> **Can we have** a coffee break?

> **Could I have** a pen, please?
> **Could I have** the key for the stationery cupboard?
> **Could I have** some more paper?

Useful words

the margin	the empty space down the side of a page
a pair	two people who are doing something together
a handout	a piece of paper containing information that is given to people in a meeting or a class
a ruler	a long, flat object that you use for measuring things and for drawing straight lines
stationery	paper, envelopes and other materials used for writing and typing

To ask if someone has something that you want, use **Have you got ... ?** .

> **Have you got** a spare textbook?
> **Have you got** any clay I can use?
> **Have you got** a copy of the new timetable?

If you need something, use **I need ...** .

> **I need** a red pen.
> **I need** some more paper.
> **I need** a calculator.

To ask someone to do something for you, use **Can you ... ?** or **Could you ... ?** .

> **Can you** give us an example?
> **Can you** repeat the instructions?
> **Can you** pass me that book?

> **Could you** repeat that, please?
> **Could you** show me how to do it?
> **Could you** help me find the books I need?

Useful words

a textbook	a book containing facts about a particular subject that is used by people studying that subject
clay	a type of earth that is soft when it is wet and hard when it is dry, and is used for making things such as pots and bricks
a timetable	a list of the times when something happens
instructions	information on how to do something
repeat	to say something again
physics	the scientific study of things such as heat, light and sound

Saying what you like, dislike, prefer

To talk about things you like, use **I like ...** .

> **I like** working in the library.
> **I like** physics.
> **I like** Mrs Kennedy's lessons.

For things you like a lot, use **I really like ...** or **I love ...** .

> **I really like** learning about computers.
> **I really like** our conversation classes.
> **I really like** the teachers here.

> **I love** learning about ancient history.
> **I love** the idea of going to university.
> **I love** discussing books in class.

For things you like doing, use **I enjoy ...** .

> **I enjoy** reading poetry.
> **I enjoy** studying languages.
> **I enjoy** meeting other students.

> **GOOD TO KNOW!**
> **Like/Enjoy + -ing**
> When **like ...** or **enjoy ...** are followed by a verb, the verb is usually in the -ing form.

To say what you do not like, use **I don't like ...** .

> **I don't like** physics.
> **I don't like** writing essays.
> **I don't like** doing homework.

Useful words

ancient history	the study of people and life from a very long time ago
poetry	the form of literature that consists of poems

Talking about your plans

We often say **I'm going to ...** to talk about what we will do in the future.

> **I'm going to** drop French next year.
> **I'm going to** do a catering course.
> **We're going to** get our teacher a present.

You can also use **I'm planning to ...** .

> **I'm planning to** go to university.
> **I'm planning to** take the exam next term.
> **I'm planning to** be a teacher.

To ask someone about their plans, use **Are you going to ... ?** .

> **Are you going to** do politics next year?
> **Are you going to** go to college?
> **Are you going to** continue your studies?

Useful words

drop	if you drop a subject, you stop studying it
catering	providing food and drinks for people
politics	the activities and ideas that are concerned with government

● Listen out for

Here are some useful phrases you may hear at school, college or university.

Turn to page 10.

Open your books at page 56.

Get into pairs.

Work in groups of 4.

Work with your partner.

Write the answers on a piece of paper.

Look it up in your dictionary.

Hand in your homework at the end of the lesson.

Put your hand up if you know the answer.

Is this all your own work?

Check your answers.

Make sure you read the questions carefully.

Put the equipment away when you have finished with it.

Useful words

your partner	a person you are doing something with
look something up	to find a fact or piece of information by looking in a book or on a computer
hand something in	to take something to someone and give it to them

---

> ### 🎧 Listen to the conversation: Track 25

Craig is at an evening class. His teacher is giving a lesson on a poem by Shakespeare.

A Good evening, everyone. Could you turn to page 26 in your textbooks? Craig, could you tell us a bit about this poem, please?

B It's a love poem.

A That's right. What do you think of it?

B I think it's very beautiful, but it's hard to understand. What does 'temperate' mean?

A It means gentle and not extreme. Why do you think Shakespeare uses this word?

B Is it because it's a word that can be used for the weather, and he is comparing his love to a summer day?

A Very good, Craig. Do you think this is a good comparison?

B I think it is, because he is saying that a summer day is very good, but his love is better than that. I don't understand the second verse, though.

A It's very difficult. I'd like you all to write down what you think it means. I'll give you 10 minutes.

B Are we allowed to work in pairs?

A Yeah, if you like. Craig, you're very good at this sort of thing. Are you planning to carry on studying after the end of this course?

B Yes, I'm going to go to university next year to do English Literature.

> ### 🎧 Listen to more phrases and practise saying them: Track 26

Glossary

gentle	kind, mild and calm
compare	to consider how things are different and how they are similar
a comparison	a study of the differences between two things
a verse	one of the groups of lines in a poem or a song

Numbers, dates and time

Three, two, one... Go!

You will often need to use numbers in conversation. You will also need to talk about the time and dates. The phrases in this unit will help you to talk about all these things with confidence.

Numbers

To say how much something costs using the unit of money that is written as €, use **... euros** and to talk about the smaller unit used with the euro, use **... cents**. For the unit of money that is written as £, use **... pounds** and for the smaller unit used with the pound, use **... pence**. For the unit of money that is written as $, use **... dollars** and for the smaller unit used with the pound, use **... cents**.

> It cost me sixty-five **euros** twenty. (€65.20)
> That'll be eighteen **dollars** and ninety-nine **cents**. ($18.99)
> He bought a bar of chocolate for eighty-nine **pence**. (89p)
> My ticket cost nine **pounds** fifty-nine. (£9.59)

To talk about how heavy something is using the units of measurement written as k and g, use **... kilos** and **... grams**. To talk about how heavy something is using the units of measurement written as lb and oz, use **... pounds** and **... ounces**.

> I'd like two **kilos** of potatoes, please.
> Can I have half a **kilo** of tomatoes?
> You need three **pounds** of apples.
> The recipe says two hundred **grams** of butter.

Useful words

cost	to have as a price
a bar	a small block of something
a recipe	a list of food and a set of instructions telling you how to cook something

To talk about how much liquid there is using the unit of measurement written as L or l, use **... litres**. For the unit of measurement written as p or pt, use **... pints**.

> I put twenty **litres** of petrol in the car.
> You need half a **litre** of milk for this recipe.
> Could you buy two **pints** of milk, please?

To talk about how long something is, using the units of measurement written as km, m and cm, use **... kilometres, ... metres** and **... centimetres**. For the units of measurement written as m, yd, ft and in, use **... miles, ... yards, ... feet** and **... inches**.

> We're thirty **kilometres** from Madrid.
> I'm one **metre** sixty-six **centimetres** tall.
> It's twenty **centimetres** long by ten wide.
> It's about eighty **miles** to Cardiff.
> He's over six **feet** tall.

To talk about amounts as parts of a hundred (%), use **... per cent**

> Fifty-five **per cent** voted no.
> The rate is two point five **per cent**.

For talking about a temperature, written as °, use **... degrees**.

> It's over thirty-five **degrees** today.

Useful words

petrol	the fuel which you use in cars and some other vehicles to make the engine go
milk	the white liquid which cows and some other animals produce, which people drink
wide	used to talk about how much something measures from one side to the other
vote	to show your choice officially at a meeting or in an election
a rate	how fast or how often something happen

To talk about the order in which something happens or comes, use **first, second, third,** etc ... .

> It's our **first** wedding anniversary today.
> This is my **second** trip to Provence.
> He came **third** in the race.

The time

Use **... o'clock** to say what time it is when the clock shows the exact hour.

> It finishes at eight **o'clock**.
> He got up this morning at five **o'clock**.
> It's one **o'clock** – time for lunch!
> It's four **o'clock** in the afternoon.

> **GOOD TO KNOW!**
> **Midday** is used to mean twelve o'clock in the middle of the day.
> **Midnight** is used to mean twelve o'clock in the middle of the night.

To say that it is thirty minutes or less after a particular hour, use **... past ...** .

> It's twenty-five **past** one.
> It's five **past** six.
> It's quarter **past** one.
> She's coming here at half **past** five.

Useful words

a wedding	a marriage ceremony and the party that often takes place after the ceremony
an anniversary	a date that is remembered because something special happened on that date in an earlier year
a trip	a journey that you make to a particular place and back again
a race	a competition to see who is the fastest
get up	to get out of bed
lunch	the meal that you have in the middle of the day
quarter past	used when you are telling the time to talk about fifteen minutes after an hour

To say that it is a particular number of minutes before a particular hour, use **... to ...** .

> It's twenty **to** one.
> It's ten **to** eight.
> I looked at my watch and it was five **to** three.
> I'm leaving at quarter **to** one.

To find out the time now or the time that something starts, use **What time ... ?**.

> **What time** is it?
> **What time**'s the next train for Manchester?
> **What time** does it start?
> **What time** shall we meet?

To say the time that something is happening, use **at ...** .

> It starts **at** seven o'clock.
> The train leaves **at** seven thirty.
> I'll see you **at** half past three.
> Let's meet up **at** quarter past five.

To say that something will happen at or before a particular time, use **by ...** .

> Can you be there **by** three o'clock?
> I have to leave **by** quarter to one.
> We have to finish this **by** quarter to one.

Useful words

quarter to   used when you are telling the time to talk about fifteen minutes
                   before an hour

● Listen out for

Here are some important phrases you may hear and use to do with the time.

> Excuse me, do you have the time, please?
> I'm sorry, I'm not wearing a watch.
> It's probably about eleven.
> I'm late.
> I must go – I'm late already.
> Did you get there on time?
> How much time do we have left?
> He should be here by now.

> The train for Paris leaves at 13:55.
> The 14:15 train to Strasbourg will depart from platform two.
> Flight number 307 for London is due to take off at 20:45.
> Flight 909 from Toronto is on time.
> The coach gets in to Sydney at 19:10.

Saying how long

If you want to say that something will happen in so many minutes' time or in so many days' time, use **in ...** .

> I'll be back **in** twenty minutes.
> She'll be here **in** a week.
> He completed the exercise **in** only three minutes.
> I can probably do the job **in** an hour or two.

Useful words

a watch	a small clock that you wear on your wrist
late	after the time that something should start or happen
on time	not late or early
depart	to leave
due	expected to happen or arrive at a particular time
take off	used for saying that an aeroplane leaves the ground and starts flying
complete	to finish a task
an exercise	an activity that you do in order to practise a skill

To ask how much time something lasts or how much time you need for something, use **How long ... ?**.

> **How long**'s the film?
> **How long** does the meeting usually last?
> **How long** will the tour take?
> **How long** will it take you to get there?

To say how much time something is needed to do something, use **It takes ...** .

> **It takes** five minutes to make.
> **It takes** about forty minutes to cook.
> **It took** two hours to walk to the village.

The seasons

To say which season, (spring, summer, autumn or winter), something happens or happened in, use **in ...** .

> We get the best weather here **in** spring.
> We don't go camping **in** winter.
> They got married **in** the summer of 1999.

Useful words

a meeting	an event in which a group of people come together to discuss things or make decisions
a tour	a trip to an interesting place or around several interesting places
cook	to prepare and heat food
weather	the temperature and conditions outside, for example if it is raining, hot or windy
camping	the activity of staying somewhere in a tent
get married	to legally become husband and wife in a special ceremony

To make it clear which spring, summer, etc. you are talking about, use **last ...** , **this ...** or **next ...** .

> We're going to Oregon **this** summer.
> I'm going to South Africa **this** winter.
> It was very cold **last** winter.
> She's expecting her baby **next** spring.

The months of the year

To say which month of the year something happens or happened in, use **in ...** .

> My birthday is **in** August.
> We'll probably go away on holiday **in** May.
> I visited some friends in Rome **in** September.
> We're going to the mountains for our holidays **in** August.

To make it clear which January or February, etc. you are talking about, use **last ...** , **this ...** or **next ...** .

> Where did you go on holiday **last** June?
> I'm hoping to go to Peru **next** July.

If you want to say which part of a month something happens in, use **at the start of ...**, **in the middle of ...** or **at the end of ...** .

> She goes to university **at the start of** October.
> The summer holidays start **at the end of** June.
> They're leaving **in the middle of** November.

Useful words

expect a baby	to have a baby growing inside you
a birthday	the day of the year that you were born
a mountain	a very high area of land with steep sides

Dates

To say what the date is, use **the first/second, etc. of March/November, etc.**
or **March/November, etc. the first/second, etc.**

> Its **the first of July** today.
> Tomorrow's **the tenth of January**.
> It's **December the third** today.
> It's **March the fifth**.

To say what date something is happening or happened on, use **on ...** before the
date.

> He was born **on** the fourteenth of February, 1990.
> He died **on** April the twenty-third, 1616.
> Barbara and Tomek got married **on** May the fifteenth.
> Where do you think you'll be **on** the twentieth of October?

GOOD TO KNOW!
To ask what the date is, use **What's the date today?** .

The days of the week

To say what day of the week it is, use **It's ...** .

> 'What day is it today?' '**It's** Thursday.'
> **It's** Wednesday today, isn't it?
> Great! **It's** Saturday today.

Useful words

be born	to come out of your mother's body and start life
die	to stop living

When saying which day something happens or will happen, use **on ...** .

I'm going to Dublin **on** Sunday.
It's my birthday **on** Tuesday.
We'll see them **on** Wednesday.
I don't work **on** Fridays.

To say what time of a particular day something happens, use **on ... morning/ afternoon/evening/night**.

I'm going to the garage **on Tuesday morning**.
I'll see you **on Friday afternoon**.
There was a good film on television **on Sunday evening**.
What are you doing **on Saturday night**?

To say that you do something all Mondays/Saturdays, etc. use **every ...** .

We call her **every** Monday.
He plays golf **every** Saturday.
I used to see them **every** Friday.
They go to the same café **every** Saturday morning.

To say that you do something one Wednesday/week, etc. and then not the next Wednesday/week, etc. and that it continues in this way, use **every other ...** .

He has the children **every other** weekend.
We play football **every other** Saturday.

Useful words

a garage   a place where you can have your car repaired
golf   a game in which you use long sticks to hit a small, hard ball into holes

To make it clear which Monday/Wednesday, etc. you are talking about, use **last ...** , **this ...** or **next ...** .

It's our wedding anniversary **this** Friday.
I'm going on holiday **this** Tuesday.
I sent you the photos **last** Friday.
Would **next** Friday be better for you?

If you want to ask what day something is happening, use **What day ... ?**.

What day's the meeting? Is it Tuesday?
Do you know **what day** he's coming?

To say what day it is today, use **It's ...** .

It's Tuesday today.
It's Friday today.

To talk about a particular time the day after today, use **tomorrow ...**

I'm seeing her **tomorrow** evening.
I've got to be up early **tomorrow** morning.
We're going to a party **tomorrow** night.

Useful words

a photo	a picture that you take with a camera
up	not in bed
a party	a social event at which people enjoy themselves doing things like eating or dancing

To talk about a particular time the day before today, use **yesterday ...** .

> It happened **yesterday** morning.
> I saw him **yesterday** afternoon.

> **GOOD TO KNOW!**
> To talk about the night that belonged to yesterday, you use **last night** and not **yesterday night**.

To say when something happened, use **... ago**.

> She called me a week **ago**.
> They left ten days **ago**.
> He was born three years **ago**.

To say how long something has been happening, use **for ...** .

> It's been raining **for** five days
> I haven't seen them **for** three weeks.
> They haven't spoken to each other **for** months.
> I've been waiting here **for** hours.
> We've been living here **for** ten months.
> I haven't seen her **for** a week.

> **GOOD TO KNOW!**
> If you want to say 'for a long time' in conversation, use **for ages**.

Useful words
it rains   water falls from the clouds in small drops

● Listen out for

Here are some important phrases you may hear and use to do with dates, months of the year and days of the week.

When's your birthday?
It's my birthday today!
It's my parents' wedding anniversary today.
When are you getting married?
When are you going on holiday?
When do you start your course?
When are you going to New Zealand?
When do you come back from New Zealand?
When is the baby due?
When was Carlo born?
Which day do you play tennis on?
Which days of the week are you free?
Is Saturday any good for you?
How about this Saturday?
I'm afraid I'm busy on Saturday.
Which month is Lena's birthday in?
Which months are the hottest?

Useful words
a course   a series of lessons on a particular subject
busy   doing something, so that you are not free to do anything else

> 🎧 **Listen to the conversation: Track 27**

Jemma and Katie are arranging to see each other.

A We could meet up for a coffee in town if you like. What are you doing this Thursday?

B Thursday is no good, I'm afraid. I'm having dinner with my boss and her husband. What about next Thursday? Are you free that afternoon?

A Oh, no, I'm away then – I'm in Sweden.

B Oh, right. When do you come back?

A On July the eleventh.

B Well, how about the Thursday after you get back – July the fourteenth.

A That's a possibility. The only problem is, I have a work meeting in the afternoon.

B How long does your meeting last?

A It'll probably finish by five o'clock. It only takes ten minutes to bike from the office to the centre of town. I could meet you in a café at around 5:30.

B Okay, great. Let's say Dino's Café at 5:30.

A Perfect!

> 🎧 **Listen to more phrases and practise saying them: Track 28**

All the phrases by function

So, to sum up ...

This unit helps you find quickly all the phrases you have learned. You will find all the phrases that are used for the same function in one place under a heading.

Contents

Agreeing and disagreeing — 205
Apologizing — 206
Asking for and giving explanations — 207
Asking for information — 207
Asking for permission — 210
Asking for things — 211
Attracting someone's attention — 213
Complaining — 213
Congratulating someone — 214
Dangers and emergencies — 215
Describing people and things — 215
Encouraging someone — 216
Explaining a problem — 217
Expressing opinions — 218
Expressing surprise — 219
Expressing sympathy — 220
Hellos and goodbyes — 220
Introducing people — 221
Making arrangements — 222
Making suggestions — 223
Making sure you've understood — 224
Please and thank you — 225
Saying what you have to do — 227
Saying what you like, dislike, prefer — 228
Saying what you want to do — 229
Talking about your health — 230
Talking about your plans — 232
Talking about yourself — 233

Agreeing and disagreeing

To agree to do something or give someone something, use **Yes** or **OK**. To make **Yes** more polite or enthusiastic, add **of course**.

> 'Will you come with me?' '**Yes**.'
> 'Could you help me with my bags?' '**Yes, of course**.'
> 'Can I have an ice cream?' '**Yes**.'
>
> 'Can you cook dinner tonight?' '**OK**, if you like.'
> 'Will you drive?' '**OK**.'
> 'Can I borrow your pen?' '**OK**.'

To say you will not do something or give someone something, use **No**.

> 'Could you give me a lift?' '**No**, sorry, I haven't got time.'
> 'Will you pay for the coffees?' '**No**, it's your turn.'

To agree with someone's opinion, use **I agree.** or **You're right.**. If you want to say who you agree with, use **with**.

> 'This is a great restaurant.' '**I agree**. We often come here.'
> **I agree with** Nigel.
> I completely **agree with you!**
>
> 'We'll be late if we don't hurry.' '**You're right** – let's go!'
> I think **you're right**.
> Matthieu**'s right**.

If you do not agree with someone's opinion, you can use **I don't think so.** .

> 'The food here's lovely, isn't it?' '**I don't think so.** My soup is much too salty.'
> 'Pierre's really nice, isn't he?' '**I don't think so.** He never speaks to me.'
> 'Travelling by train is really relaxing.' '**I don't think so.** I prefer to fly.'

Apologizing

To apologize, use **I'm sorry ...** or **Sorry ...** .

> **I'm sorry** – I've forgotten your name.
> **I'm sorry** – I've forgotten to bring those figures with me.
> **I'm sorry** I'm late.

> **Sorry** – I have to leave now.
> **Sorry**, I didn't hear what you were saying.
> **Sorry**, I didn't introduce you.

If you have to tell someone that there is a problem or that something bad has happened, start your sentence with **I'm afraid ...** .

> **I'm afraid** I'm going to be late.
> **I'm afraid** I can't come tonight.
> **I'm afraid** there's a problem with your order.

If someone says sorry to you, you can make them feel better by saying **It doesn't matter.** or **Don't worry about it.** .

> 'I'm sorry – I've spilled your drink.' '**It doesn't matter**.'
> 'Sorry we're late.' '**It doesn't matter** – I've only just got here myself.'

> 'Sorry I forgot your birthday.' '**Don't worry about it**.'
> 'I'm afraid the handle's come off the door.' '**Don't worry about it** – it happens all the time.'

A more informal way to tell someone that something does not matter is **No worries.** or **That's OK.** .

> 'Sorry I can't come to your party.' '**No worries**, I understand.'
> 'We've eaten all the food.' '**No worries**. I'm not hungry.'

> 'Sorry about the noise.' '**That's OK** – it didn't bother me.'
> 'I didn't bring a coat.' '**That's OK** – I can lend you one.'

Asking for and giving explanations

The simplest way to ask for an explanation is to use **Why ... ?** .

> **Why** do I need to heat the liquid?
> **Why** are there no women poets on this list?
> **Why** can't fish breathe out of water?

Could you explain ... ? can be used to ask someone to explain something.

> **Could you explain** why the flame changes colour?
> **Could you explain** what happens when the cell divides?
> **Could you explain** how to do this calculation?

To ask for a reason, use **What is the reason ... ?**.

> **What is the reason** that birds fly south in winter?
> **What is the reason** for the change in temperature?
> **What is the reason** for Juliet's happiness?

To give an explanation, use **Because ...** .

> **Because** he was working in Paris at that time.
> Your answer was not correct **because** you put the decimal point in the wrong place.
> **Because** he was not able to write any more.

Asking for information

To ask for information, use the question words **Where ... ?**, **When ... ?**, **Why ... ?**, **Who ... ?**, **Which ... ?**, **What ... ?**, and **How ... ?**.

> **Where** is your office?
> **Where** do you work?

> **When** did you meet Olga?
> **When** is his party?

Why did you decide to become a teacher?
Why did you leave Tokyo?

Who did you see last time?
Who is your doctor?

Which brand do you recommend?
Which batteries do I need to buy for my camera?

What's the name of the hotel?
What's the landlord's address?

How can we find a plumber?
How do I turn the computer on?

Use **Tell me ...** for general questions about someone's life.

Tell me about your family.
Tell me a bit about yourself.
Tell me about your work.

To ask someone to describe someone or something use **What's ... like?** .

What's your course **like**?
What's his new girlfriend **like**?
What's your hotel **like**?

We often start questions that ask for information with **Is ... ?** .

Is it expensive?
Is it far from the city centre?
Is breakfast included in the price?

To ask questions about something, especially in a shop, use **Is this ... ?** or **Is it ... ?** .

Is this the only model you have?
Is this the biggest size?
Are these the only colours you have?

Is it made of real leather?
Is it big enough for four people?
Is it free?

To ask if a place has something, use **Is there ... ?**, or **Are there any ... ?** .

Is there a hairdryer in the room?
Is there a TV?
Is there much noise from the neighbours?

Are there any good schools near here?
Are there any rules about having guests to stay?
Are there any more blankets?

You could also use **Does ... have ... ?** .

Does the flat **have** central heating?
Does the hotel **have** a swimming pool?
Does it **have** a garden?

To ask how to do something, use **How do you ... ?** .

How do you get to the old town?
How do you buy tickets?
How do you know which bus to catch?

To ask about time, use **What time ... ?** .

What time's dinner?
What time does he get home?
What time do we have to leave in the morning?

To ask about prices, use **How much ... ?** .

How much is a double room per night?
How much rent do you pay?
How much do you charge for breakfast?

To ask about the time that something will take, use **How long ... ?**.

> **How long** does the tour last?
> **How long** is the boat trip?
> **How long** does it take to get there?

Asking for permission

To ask for permission, use **Can I ... ?**.

> **Can I** see the room?
> **Can I** pay by credit card?
> **Can we** camp here?

To check if you can do something, use **Am I allowed to ... ?**.

> **Am I allowed to** use the washing machine?
> **Am I allowed to** have guests?
> **Are we allowed to** ask questions?

To make sure you will not upset someone, use **Do you mind if ... ?**.

> **Do you mind if** I park my car here for a moment?
> **Do you mind if** I leave my suitcase here for five minutes?
> **Do you mind if** we look at the rooms before we decide?

A slightly informal way of asking for permission is **Is it OK to ... ?**.

> **Is it OK to** look inside the box?
> **Is it OK to** try one of your oranges?
> **Is it OK to** take the alarm clock out of its box?

Asking for things

To ask for something, use **Can I have ... ?** or **Could I have ... ?**. To be polite, use **please** at the beginning or end of the question.

> **Can I have** two tickets, **please**?
> **Can I have** your guidebook for a minute?
> **Can I have** an audio guide, **please**?

> **Could I have** the key to my room, please?
> **Could I have** a receipt, please?
> **Please could I have** two more towels?

To say what you want, use **I'd like ...** .

> **I'd like** a double room, please.
> **I'd like** to stay three nights.
> **I'd like** a flat near the university.

To describe the thing you want, use **I'm looking for ...** or **I want ...** .

> **I'm looking for** a room in a shared house.
> **I'm looking for** a place to rent.
> **We're looking for** a house with four bedrooms.

> **I want** a house with a large garden.
> **I want** to rent a house for six months.
> **I want** a room with a view of the sea.

If it is important for you to have something, you can use **I need ...** .

> **I need** the address of the museum.
> **She needs** two more tickets.
> **We need** a guide who can speak English.

To ask if a shop sells the thing you want, use **Do you sell ... ?**.

> **Do you sell** light bulbs?
> **Do you sell** fruit?
> **Do you sell** newspapers?

To ask if a shop sells the thing you want or if someone has the thing you want, use **Have you got ... ?** .

> **Have you got** any strawberries?
> **Have you got** a spare textbook?
> **Have you got** a copy of the new timetable?

When you have decided what you want to buy in a shop, use **I'll have ...** or **I'll take ...** .

> **I'll have** a strawberry ice cream.
> **I'll have** the red one.
> **I'll have** 200 grams of ham.

> **I'll take** these two postcards.
> **I'll take** the blue ones.
> **I'll take** two pineapples.

If you are asking someone if they can do something for you, use **Can you ... ?** or **Could you ... ?** . **Could you ... ?** is slightly more polite and formal than **Can you ...?** . To be polite, use **please** at the beginning or end of these sentences.

> **Can you** tell me what the opening hours are?
> **Can you** give me directions to the Science Museum?
> **Please can you** show me where we are on this map?

> **Could you** show me the room, **please**?
> **Could you** get someone to repair the window?
> **Could you** call a taxi for me, **please**?

Can I ... ? is also used in sentences where you are asking if something you want to do is possible. If you want to be very polite, you can use **Is it possible to ... ?** .

> **Can I** see the dentist this morning?
> **Can I** talk to a nurse?
> **Can I** drive while I'm taking this medicine?

> **Is it possible to** see a different doctor?
> **Is it possible to** get an earlier appointment?
> **Is it possible to** meet the surgeon before my operation?

Attracting someone's attention

When you are asking for information you may need to get someone's attention before you can ask them a question. To do this, first say **excuse me**.

> **Excuse me**, is the modern art museum near here?
> **Excuse me**, do you know what time the gardens open?
> **Excuse me**, where do I buy a ticket?

Complaining

A simple way to start a sentence explaining what it wrong is with **It's ...** .

> **It's** very cold in my room.
> **It's** too expensive.
> **It's** not big enough.

To talk about an event or an activity that is now over, use **It was ...** .

> **It was** really expensive.
> **It was** a waste of money.
> **It was** difficult to find.

To talk about something that should not be there, use **There's ...** .

> **There's** too much noise.
> **There's** dirt all over the floor.
> **There's** a damp patch on the wall.

If you think you should have something that you do not have, use **There isn't ...** .

> **There isn't** any hot water.
> **There isn't** anywhere to keep my bike.
> **There isn't** enough room to study.

If something is not good enough, use **I'm not happy with ...** .

> **I'm not happy with** the food.
> **I'm not happy with** my room.
> **I'm not happy with** the way the place is cleaned.

Congratulating someone

To show that you are pleased that something good has happened to someone, use **Congratulations!**.

> **Congratulations** on your new job!
> **Congratulations** on the birth of your baby son!
> You passed your exam? **Congratulations!**

To show that you think someone has done something very well, use **Well done!** .

> **Well done**, Mercedes!
> 'I got that job, by the way.' **'Well done!** That's great!'
> 'Look, I've tidied up all those papers.' **'Well done!'**

Dangers and emergencies

To ask for help because you are in danger, shout **Help!** .

> **Help!** I can't swim!
> **Help!** The building's on fire!

To tell someone that they are in danger, shout **Look out!** or say **Be careful**.

> **Look out!** There's a car coming!
> **Look out!** It's falling!

> **Be careful** on those steps!
> **Be careful!** It's icy outside.

Describing people and things

Start general descriptions of things with **It's ...** and of people with **He's/She's ...** .

> **It's** gold with three diamonds.
> **It's** a ladies' watch.
> **It's** a green suitcase with wheels.

> **He's** five years old.
> **She's** eight.
> **He was** about sixty.

Use **It's made of ...** to say what something is made of.

> **It's made of** leather.
> It's quite a small bag, and **it's made of** velvet.
> The beads are bright blue and **they're made of** glass.

Use **He's/She's got ...** to talk about what someone looks like.

> **She's got** short blond hair.
> **He's got** a beard.
> **She's got** a big nose.

To talk about someone's clothes, use **He's/She's wearing ...** .

> **She's wearing** jeans and a green T-shirt.
> **She's wearing** an orange blouse.
> **He's wearing** a black jacket.

Encouraging someone

To encourage someone to go somewhere more quickly or to do something more quickly, use **Hurry up!** .

> **Hurry up!** We've got to be there in ten minutes!
> **Hurry up!** We're late already!
> **Hurry up**, Mario! When you've finished your work, you can go out to play.

To encourage someone to go somewhere or to do something more quickly, you can also use **Come on!** .

> **Come on**, Helena, or we'll be late!
> **Come on!** We're going to miss our train!
> **Come on!** We haven't got all day!
> **Come on!** Have a swim with us. The water's lovely!

To encourage someone to do something, you can use **Go for it!** . **Go for it!** is slightly informal.

> 'I'm thinking of applying for that job.' '**Go for it!**'
> 'I've decided I want to run a marathon.' '**Go for it!**'
> 'I'd like to go and see Paolo in New York.' '**Go for it!**'

Explaining a problem

To explain a general problem, use **I've got a problem ...** . Use the preposition **with** to talk about a thing that is causing your problem.

> **I've got a problem** – I want to study French and Italian but the classes are at the same time.
> **I've got a problem** – this homework has to be done by tomorrow, but I haven't got the books I need.
> **I've got a problem with** my presentation – it's far too long and I don't know what to cut out.
> **I've got a problem with** my central heating.

If you are asking somebody for help, you will need to be able to describe the problem. Use **There's ...** to say what the problem is.

> **There's** a smell of gas in my room.
> **There's** a noise coming from the engine.
> **There are** mice in the kitchen.

If the problem is that you do not have something you need, use **There isn't ...** or **I haven't got ...** .

> **There isn't** any soap in the bathroom.
> **There isn't** enough food for everyone.
> **There aren't** any towels in my room.

> **I haven't got** her address.
> **She hasn't got** enough money.
> **He hasn't got** a car.

For some problems, you can use **I've got ...** .

> **I've got** a problem.
> **I've got** a flat tyre.
> **I've got** too much work.

If the problem is that you are not able to do something, use **I can't ...** .

> **I can't** drive.
> **We can't** open the bedroom door.
> **I can't** find my keys.

If you want to say that you do not understand something, use **I don't understand ...** .

> **I don't understand** what he's saying.
> **I don't understand** the instructions.
> **I don't understand** how to use this phone.

Expressing opinions

To express your opinions, use **I think ...** .

> **I think** Sonia's right.
> I really **think** it's too late to go to the cinema.
> **I think** it's a great idea.

If you do not think something is true, use **I don't think ...** .

> **I don't think** Marc's coming.
> **I don't think** we should stay much longer.
> **I don't think** the restaurant is open on Mondays.

If you want to ask other people if they think something is good or bad, use **What do you think of ... ?** .

> **What do you think of** his latest movie?
> **What do you think of** this idea?
> **What do you think of** Mira's new boyfriend?

To ask someone if they think something is a good idea, use **What do you think about ... ?** .

> **What do you think about** going out for dinner tonight?
> **What do you think about** inviting Eva?
> **What do you think about** having a party at the weekend?

If you are trying to choose between two or more things and you want an opinion from the person you are with, use **Which ... ?** .

> **Which** one do you like best?
> **Which** dress shall I buy?
> **Which** skirt fits best?

Expressing surprise

A simple way to show that you are surprised by what someone has said is to use **Really?** .

> 'Zareb is leaving?' **'Really?** Why?'
> 'I don't think it's a very good school.' **'Really?** I was very impressed by it.'
> 'I'm really bad at maths?' **'Really?** I can't believe that!'

A stronger way to show that you are surprised by what someone has said is to say **That's incredible!** or **That's amazing!** .

> You ran twenty miles in two and a half hours? **That's incredible!**
> So he works a sixty-hour week? **That's incredible!**
>
> She spent two thousand pounds on a jacket? **That's amazing!**
> You cooked for sixty people? **That's amazing!**

Expressing sympathy

The most common way to show that you are sad for someone when something bad has happened is to use **I'm sorry to hear ...** .

> **I'm** so **sorry to hear** that your mother died.
> **I'm sorry to hear** that Charlie has lost his job, Sara.
> **I'm sorry to hear** you didn't get the house you wanted.

To show that you are sorry when something slightly bad or disappointing has happened, use **It's a shame ...** .

> **It's a shame** you couldn't come with us last night.
> **It's a shame** she didn't pass her exam after all that hard work.
> **It's a shame** so few people came to the concert.

Hellos and goodbyes

Use **Hello ...** as a general greeting. It is polite to say **hello** to anyone in any situation.

> **Hello** Jorge.
> **Hello** Dr Ahmed.

Use **Hi ...** in informal situations, for example when you are meeting friends.

> **Hi**, how are things with you?
> **Hi**, how are you doing?
> Oh **hi** Adam, I didn't know you were coming.

Use **Good morning, Good afternoon** or **Good evening** in slightly more formal situations, for instance if you meet a neighbour, or when you see people at work.

> **Good morning** everyone. Today we are going to be looking at how to form questions.
> **Good afternoon** Mr Kowalski.

Use **Goodbye ...** when you leave someone.

> **Goodbye** Dwight, have a safe journey.

Goodbye ... is often shortened to **Bye ...** .

> **Bye** everyone!

Use **Goodnight ...** when you are going to bed, or if someone else is going to bed.

> **Goodnight** everyone – see you in the morning.

See you ... is a rather informal way of saying goodbye to someone you know you will see again.

> OK, I need to go now. **See you!**
> **See you** tomorrow!
> **See you** on Monday!

If someone has come to a place for the first time, you could say **Welcome!** .

> **Welcome!** I'm so pleased you could come.
> **Welcome** to the UK!
> **Welcome** to Vancouver!

Introducing people

If you want to introduce someone to someone else, use **This is ...** . To introduce a group of people, use **These are ...** .

> **This is** my husband, Richard.
> **This is** Medina, my friend from school.

> **These are** my children, Andrew, Gordon and Emma.
> **These are** my parents.

> **GOOD TO KNOW!**
> When you are introduced to someone, you can just say **Hello**, or in a
> slightly more formal situation, say **Pleased to meet you**.

Making arrangements

To make an arrangement, use **We can ...** .

> **We can** have lunch in town.
> **We can** meet this evening.
> **We can** travel together.

To explain an arrangement, use **I'll ...** .

> **I'll** meet you outside the cinema.
> **I'll** pick you up at seven.
> **I'll** text you when I'm ready.

To ask someone about the place they want to meet, use **Where ... ?**.

> **Where** shall we meet?
> **Where** shall we go to eat?
> **Where** would you like to eat?

To ask someone about the time they want to meet, use **When ... ?** or
What time ... ?.

> **When** shall we eat?
> **When** do you want to meet for dinner?
> **When** do you want to have dinner?

> **What time** shall we meet?
> **What time** would you like to meet?
> **What time** would you like to eat?

To check if someone is happy with an arrangement, use **Is ... OK?** .

> **Is** eight o'clock **OK?**
> **Is** a pizza **OK?**
> **Is** it **OK** to bring Charlie?

To ask what the best arrangement is, use **Is it better to ... ?**.

> **Is it better to** meet outside the restaurant?
> **Is it better to** book a table?
> **Is it better to** arrive early?

Making suggestions

One easy way of making suggestions is to use **We could ...**

> **We could** ask Paul to join us.
> **We could** meet another time.
> **We could** meet at the Café de la Poste.

To suggest what someone else can do, use **You could ...** .

> **You could** go on a tour of the city.
> **You could** ask Janne to show you the old town .
> **You could** take the children to the fair.

If you are keen to do something, you could say **Let's ...** .

> **Let's** buy some flowers.
> **Let's** get the expensive one – it will be much better.
> **Let's** choose some new bedclothes.

If you want to make a suggestion and see if other people agree with you, use **Shall we ... ?** .

> **Shall we** see what Valerio wants to do?
> **Shall we** order a pizza?
> **Shall we** ask Suri if she wants to come with us?

If you have an idea about something you could do, use **How about ... ?** .

> **How about** going swimming?
> **How about** asking for some time off work?
> **How about** sending him a text?

Making sure you've understood

If you do not understand what someone has said, use **I don't understand.** .

> Sorry, **I don't understand.**
> **I don't understand** what you said.
> Please could you repeat that? **I didn't understand**.

You can ask for help with understanding by using **Would you mind ... ?** .

> **Would you mind** speaking more slowly?
> **Would you mind** repeating that?
> **Would you mind** speaking in English?

To check the meaning of a word, use **What does ... mean?** .

> **What does** 'fragile' **mean**?
> **What does** 'end up' **mean**?
> **What does** 'out of order' **mean**?

GOOD TO KNOW!
If you do not hear what someone has said and you want them to repeat it, use **Pardon?** or **Sorry?**.

Please and thank you

When asking for something from someone, use **please**.

> Two kilos of oranges, **please**.
> A large apple tart, **please**.
> Could you give these to Anders, **please**?
> **Please** could I borrow this chair?
> **Please** could you tidy up now?

To say that you would like something that someone has offered you, use **Yes, please.** .

> 'Would you like some more coffee?' '**Yes, please**.'
> 'Do you need a bag?' '**Yes, please**.'
> 'Can I help you with those bags?' 'Oh, **yes, please**.'
> 'Would you like me to post this for you?' '**Yes, please**.'

To thank someone, use **Thank you** or **Thanks**. **Thanks** is slightly informal.

> **Thank you** for all your help, Zalika.
> **Thank you** very much for coming here tonight.
> 'Here's a little birthday present.' '**Thank you!**'
> 'You look lovely in that dress.' '**Thank you**, Judy.'

> **GOOD TO KNOW!**
> To make **Thank you** or **Thanks** stronger, use **very much** after it.

> 'Here, have a cup of coffee.' '**Thanks**, Roman.'
> 'I love your new haircut.' '**Thanks**, Juliana.'
> Hey, **thanks** for helping out at the weekend, Anneli. I really appreciate it.
> **Thanks** very much for all those books you gave us. It was very kind of you.

> **GOOD TO KNOW!**
> People often say something extra after saying **thank you** or **thanks**
> to make it stronger. For example they often say **I appreciate it** or
> **It was a great help**. They also sometimes say **It was very kind of you**.

To accept someone's thanks, use **You're welcome.** or **Not at all.** .

> 'Thank you very much for all your help, John. We do appreciate it.'
> '**You're welcome**.'
> 'Thanks for dinner last night. It was really lovely.' '**You're welcome**.
> Any time.'

> 'Thanks for looking after the children on Saturday – that was a great
> help, Lucia.' '**Not at all**.'
> 'Thank you for lending me the book. I loved it.' '**Not at all**.'

Another way of accepting someone's thanks is to use **It's my pleasure.** or
My pleasure. This is a slightly more formal way of accepting thanks.

> 'Thank you for the lovely gifts.' '**It's my pleasure**.'
> 'Thank you very much for your cheque. It was very kind of you, Charlotte.'
> '**It's my pleasure**.'

> 'Thank you, Simone.' '**My pleasure.**'
> 'Thank you, Ben – you've been a great help.' '**My pleasure.**'

To accept thanks from a person that you know, use **That's all right.** .

> 'Thanks for your help, mate.' '**That's all right**.'
> 'A present for me? Thanks, Patrick.' '**That's all right**.'

Another way of accepting thanks from a person that you know is to use
No problem. .

> 'Thanks for looking after Rosie – it was a great help.' '**No problem**.'
> 'Thanks for the party invitation.' '**No problem**.'

Saying what you have to do

To tell people what you have to do, use **I have to ...** or **I've got to ...** .

> **I have to** make a phone call.
> **I have to** stay in tonight.
> **We have to** be there at eight o'clock.

> **I've got to** buy a present for Max.
> **I've got to** get a new toothbrush.
> **I've got to** replace my old laptop.

To ask what someone has to do, use **Do you have to ... ?** .

> **Do you have to** give them an answer today?
> **Do you have to** go now?
> **Do we have to** bring something?

To say what you have to do in a strong way, use **I must** .

> **I must** finish this work today.
> **I must** warn them.
> **I must** pay him back this week.

When you want to say that you should or ought to do something, use **I should ...** .

> **I should** call Anne.
> **You should** come and visit us.
> **I should** give you my mobile number.

You could also use **I need to ...** .

> **I need to** get some apples.
> **I need to** buy a tent.
> **I need to** get a new pair of glasses.

If something is important, you could use **It is important for me to ...** .

> **It is important for me to** pass this exam.
> **It is important for me to** find my notes.
> **It is important for me to** work as hard as possible.

Saying what you like, dislike, prefer

To talk about what you like, use **I like ...** .

> **I like** small hotels.
> **I like** campsites in the mountains.
> **I like** this guest house.

If you like something very much, use **I really like ...** or **I love ...** .

> **I really like** living here.
> **I really like** your sofa.
> **I really like** being so close to my work.

> **I love** modern furniture.
> **I love** the peace of the countryside.
> **I love** living on my own.

If you like something, but not in a strong way, use **I quite like ...** .

> **I quite like** going to films.
> **I quite like** the ballet.
> **I quite like** exploring new places.

For things you like doing, use **I enjoy ...** .

> **I enjoy** reading poetry.
> **I enjoy** studying languages.
> **I enjoy** meeting other students.

If you do not like something, use **I don't like ...** .

> **I don't like** this hotel.
> **I don't like** living with my brother.
> **I don't like** this style of building.

To say very strongly that you do not like something, use **I hate ...** .

> **I hate** being late.
> **I hate** horror movies.
> **I hate** travelling by underground.

If you want to say that you like one thing more than another, use **I prefer ...** .
If you want to talk about the thing you like less, use **to** before it.

> **I prefer** youth hostels **to** camping.
> **I prefer** living alone.
> **I prefer** this town **to** my home town.

You can also use **I like ... more than ...** .

> **I like** the pink one **more than** the red one.
> **I like** the plastic cups **more than** the glass ones.
> **I like** orange juice **more than** apple juice.

Saying what you want to do

To talk about what you would like to do, use **I'd like to ...** or **I want to ...** .

> **I'd like to** talk to him about Spain.
> **I'd like to** meet your brother.
> **We'd like to** take you out for a drink.

> **I want to** leave by 5 this afternoon.
> **I want to** speak to her as soon as possible.
> **I want to** invite you all for dinner.

If you know that you do not want to do something, use **I don't want to ...** .

    I don't want to stay in this room.
    I don't want to leave my car here.
    We don't want to go to the hotel without our luggage.

If you are very eager to do something, use **I'd really like to ...** or **I'd love to ...** .

    I'd really like to see the Great Wall of China.
    I'd really like to take the children to the beach.
    I'd really like to take some photos of the town.

    I'd love to go to the cinema.
    I'd love to go walking in the mountains.
    I'd love to visit the palace.

Use **I'd prefer to ...** when you want to do one thing and not another.

    I'd prefer to go to a local hospital.
    I'd prefer to see a female doctor.
    I'd prefer to drive there.

You can talk about things that it is important for you to do by using **I need to ...** .

    I need to buy a dictionary.
    You need to see a doctor.
    I need to go to the pharmacy.

Talking about your health

After saying hello to someone, especially someone we know, we usually ask about their health, by saying **How are you?** .

    Hello, Jan. **How are you?**
    It's great to see you, Anna. **How are you?**

> **GOOD TO KNOW!**
> To answer that question, use **I'm fine, thanks.** or **I'm good thanks.** .
> If you are not well, you could say **Not great, really.** or **Not too good, actually.** .

If you need to describe a medical problem, you can use **I've got ...** .

> **I've got** a temperature.
> **I've got** a cold.
> **I've got** asthma.

If you want to say which part of your body hurts, use **my ... hurts**.

> **My** back **hurts**.
> **His** foot **hurts**.
> **My** neck **hurts**.

If the pain you have is an ache, you can say which part of your body it is in by using **I've got ... ache**.

> **I've got** a head**ache**.
> **I've got** stomach **ache**.
> **She's got** tooth**ache**.

You can talk about more general problems that you are having using **I feel ...** .

> **I feel** tired all the time.
> **I feel** sick.
> **I feel** better now.

Talking about your plans

To tell people about your plans, use **I'm going to ...** or **I'll ...** .

> **I'm going to** phone him.
> **I'm going to** tell him I can't come.
> **I'm going to** have lunch with Ted.

> **I'll** be staying for a week.
> **I'll** pay the rent in advance.
> **We'll** arrive in the evening.

To ask someone about their plans, use **Are you going to ... ?** or **Will you ... ?** .

> **Are you going to** go to the concert?
> **Are you going to** look for a new job?
> **Are you going to** get a taxi home?

> **Will you** spend all day at the museum?
> **Will you** have time to see the gardens?
> **Will you** take your camera with you?

You can tell people about your plans using **I'm planning to ...** .

> **I'm planning to** buy a flat near the river.
> **I'm planning to** rent a room in a colleague's house.
> **I'm planning to** move to London.

To talk about what you're thinking of doing, use **I'm thinking of ...** .

> **I'm thinking of** going to the market tomorrow.
> **I'm thinking of** going shopping in Paris.
> **I'm thinking of** buying a new car.

For something you would like to do, but that is not certain, use **I hope to ...** .

> **I hope to** find something for under 20 euros.
> **I hope to** get a cheap sofa in the sales.
> **We hope to** find a present for Laurent.

Talking about yourself

When you are talking to people, you will probably want to tell them some things about you. To say what your name is, use **I'm ...** or, in a slightly more formal situation, **My name's ...** .

> Hi, **I'm** Tariq – I'm a friend of Susie.
> **I'm** Paul – I'm your teacher for this week.
>
> **My name's** Johann.
> **My name's** Yuko – I'm Kazuo's sister.

If you want to say how old you are, use **I'm ...** . You can just say a number, or you can add **... years old** after the number.

> **I'm** twenty-two.
> **I'm** thirty-seven **years old**.

To give general information about yourself, use **I'm ...** .

> **I'm** a friend of Paolo's.
> **I'm** married with two children.
> **I'm** interested in old cars.

To talk about your work, use **I'm a ...** with the name of a job, or **I work ...** to say something more general about what you do.

> **I'm a** doctor.
> **I'm a** bus driver.

> **I work** for an oil company.
> **I work** in Paris.
> **I work** as a translator.

> **GOOD TO KNOW!**
> If you want to ask someone what their job is, use **What do you do?**.

To talk about where you live, use **I live ...** or **I'm from ...** . **I'm from ...** is also used to talk about where you were born and lived as a child, even if you do not live there now.

> **I live** in Wales.
> **We live** near Moscow.

> **I'm from** Poland, but I live in Paris now.
> **We're from** Newcastle.

Grammar

Irregular verbs

Regular verbs form the present simple tense for he/she/it by adding **-s**,
the present participle by adding **-ing**, and the past simple tense and
the past participle by adding **-ed** to the base form.

| **walk** | walks | walking | walked | walked |

Irregular verbs do not behave in this way. Here are some of the most useful
irregular verbs.

base verb	he/she/it present	present participle (-ing form)	past simple	past participle
be	is	being	was/were	been
bear	bears	bearing	bore	borne
beat	beats	beating	beat	beaten
become	becomes	becoming	became	become
begin	begins	beginning	began	begun
bend	bends	bending	bent	bent
bet	bets	betting	bet	bet
bite	bites	biting	bit	bitten
bleed	bleeds	bleeding	bled	bled
blow	blows	blowing	blew	blown
break	breaks	breaking	broke	broken
bring	brings	bringing	brought	brought
build	builds	building	built	built
burn	burns	burning	burnt/burned	burnt/burned
burst	bursts	bursting	burst	burst
buy	buys	buying	bought	bought
catch	catches	catching	caught	caught
choose	chooses	choosing	chose	chosen
come	comes	coming	came	come
cost	costs	costing	cost	cost
cut	cuts	cutting	cut	cut
deal	deals	dealing	dealt	dealt
dig	digs	digging	dug	dug
draw	draws	drawing	drew	drawn
dream	dreams	dreaming	dreamt/dreamed	dreamt/dreamed

drink	drinks	drinking	drank	drunk
drive	drives	driving	drove	driven
eat	eats	eating	ate	eaten
fall	falls	falling	fell	fallen
feed	feeds	feeding	fed	fed
feel	feels	feeling	felt	felt
fight	fights	fighting	fought	fought
find	finds	finding	found	found
fly	flies	flying	flew	flown
forget	forgets	forgetting	forgot	forgotten
forgive	forgives	forgiving	forgave	forgiven
freeze	freezes	freezing	froze	frozen
get	gets	getting	got	got
give	gives	giving	gave	given
go	goes	going	went	gone
grow	grows	growing	grew	grown
hang	hangs	hanging	hung	hung
have	has	having	had	had
hear	hears	hearing	heard	heard
hide	hides	hiding	hid	hidden
hit	hits	hitting	hit	hit
hold	holds	holding	held	held
hurt	hurts	hurting	hurt	hurt
keep	keeps	keeping	kept	kept
kneel	kneels	kneeling	knelt/kneeled	knelt/kneeled
know	knows	knowing	knew	known
lay	lays	laying	laid	laid
lead	leads	leading	led	led
lean	leans	leaning	leant	leant
learn	learns	learning	learnt/learned	learnt/learned
leave	leaves	leaving	left	left
lend	lends	lending	lent	lent
let	lets	letting	let	let
lie = body position	lies	lying	lay	lain
lie = say false thing	lies	lying	lied	lied
light	lights	lighting	lit/lighted	lit/lighted
lose	loses	losing	lost	lost
make	makes	making	made	made
mean	means	meaning	meant	meant

meet	meets	meeting	met	met
pay	pays	paying	paid	paid
put	puts	putting	put	put
quit	quits	quitting	quit	quit
read	reads	reading	read	read
ride	rides	riding	rode	ridden
ring	rings	ringing	rang	rung
rise	rises	rising	rose	risen
run	runs	running	ran	run
say	says	saying	said	said
see	sees	seeing	saw	seen
sell	sells	selling	sold	sold
send	sends	sending	sent	sent
set	sets	setting	set	set
sew	sews	sewing	sewed	sewn/sewed
shake	shakes	shaking	shook	shaken
shine	shines	shining	shone	shone
shoot	shoots	shooting	shot	shot
show	shows	showing	showed	shown/showed
shrink	shrinks	shrinking	shrank	shrunk
shut	shuts	shutting	shut	shut
sing	sings	singing	sang	sung
sink	sinks	sinking	sank	sunk
sit	sits	sitting	sat	sat
sleep	sleeps	sleeping	slept	slept
slide	slides	sliding	slid	slid
smell	smells	smelling	smelled/smelt	smelled/smelt
speak	speaks	speaking	spoke	spoken
spell	spells	spelling	spelled/spelt	spelled/spelt
spend	spends	spending	spent	spent
spill	spills	spilling	spilled/spilt	spilled/spilt
spin	spins	spinning	spun	spun
spit	spits	spitting	spat	spat
split	splits	splitting	split	split
spoil	spoils	spoiling	spoiled/spoilt	spoiled/spoilt
spread	spreads	spreading	spread	spread
stand	stands	standing	stood	stood
steal	steals	stealing	stole	stolen
stick	sticks	sticking	stuck	stuck
sting	stings	stinging	stung	stung
swear	swears	swearing	swore	sworn

sweep	sweeps	sweeping	swept	swept
swim	swims	swimming	swam	swum
swing	swings	swinging	swung	swung
take	takes	taking	took	taken
teach	teaches	teaching	taught	taught
tear	tears	tearing	tore	torn
tell	tells	telling	told	told
think	thinks	thinking	thought	thought
throw	throws	throwing	threw	thrown
understand	understands	understanding	understood	understood
upset	upsets	upsetting	upset	upset
wake	wakes	waking	woke	woken
wear	wears	wearing	wore	worn
win	wins	winning	won	won
wind	winds	winding	wound	wound
write	writes	writing	wrote	written

Verb tenses

The present simple

The present simple tense is used for things that happen regularly or things that are always true. It is also used to show the speaker's opinions or beliefs.

They often **go** to the cinema on Saturdays.
He **watches** a lot of TV.
I **like** coffee for breakfast.
The sun **rises** in the east.
They **live** in Canada.
I **think** he's a very good teacher.

The present continuous

We use the present continuous to talk about things that are happening now, at the time when we are talking.

> I can't come out – I'm **doing** my homework.
> She's **staying** with friends for two weeks.

We also use the present continuous to talk about arrangements for future events.

> I'm **flying** to New York next week.
> I'm **seeing** Milos tonight.

The past simple

The past simple tense is used for single actions in the past.

> I **met** Charlotte in the café.
> We **walked** around the park.

It is also used for repeated actions in the past, often with *always*, *never* or *often*.

> I often **had** lunch with her.
> We always **sent** each other birthday cards.

The present perfect

The present perfect is used to talk about things that happened or were done and completed in the past, but which have some connection with the present. When you use the present perfect, you do not mention a specific time.

> Her daughter **has had** an accident.
> They **have bought** their tickets.
> **Have** you **bought** your tickets yet?

The past continuous

The past continuous is used to talk about things that began in the past but were not finished, or that were interrupted. It is often used with specific times.

> What **were** you **doing** at eight o'clock last night?
> I **was waiting** for a bus.
> We **were sitting** in the kitchen when Dad came in.

The future simple

The future simple is used to talk about things in the future.

> I **will come** and see you tomorrow.
> She**'ll phone** you later.
> They**'ll eat** at the restaurant.

Forming questions

Word order in questions

In statements, the subject usually comes before the first verb, but in questions it comes after the verb.

> His bedroom is big. > Is his bedroom big?
> The weather was good. > Was the weather good?
> The hotel is near here. > Is the hotel near here?

Using the verb 'be' to make questions

Be is used to make questions asking someone to describe something.
For questions in the present tense use **Is ... ?** for singular things and **Are ... ?**
for plural things. For questions about what things were like in the past,
use **Was ... ?** for singular things and **Were ... ?** for plural things.

> **Is** she tall?
> **Are** they very rich?
> **Was** the food good?
> **Were** your parents pleased?

Be is also used for making questions to ask if something exists or is in a place.
For questions in the present tense use **Is there ... ?** for singular things and
Are there ... ? for plural things. For questions about what things were like
in the past, use **Was there ... ?** for singular things and **Were there ... ?**
for plural things.

> **Is there** a cinema in your town?
> **Are there** any more chairs?
> **Was there** much noise?
> **Were there** many people there?

Using auxiliary verbs to make questions

The auxiliary verbs in English are **be**, **have**, and **do**. They are used to make
questions in just the same way that they are used to form the different tenses,
explained above.

We use **do** or **does** to make questions in the present simple, and **did** to make
questions in the past simple.

> **Do** you like cheese?
> **Do** they want to come with us?
> **Does** she have enough money?
> **Does** it cost a lot?

Did you see the elephants?
Did they do their homework?
Did we win?
Did he lock the door?

We use **am**, **are** or **is** to make questions in the present continuous, and **was** or **were** to make questions in the past continuous.

Am I doing this right?
Are you working at the moment?
Is he eating his food?
Is your mum coming?

Was he talking to Jim?
Was the car working OK?
Were the children playing in the park?
Were they helping?

We use **has** or **have** to make questions in the present perfect.

Has the parcel arrived yet?
Has Marc finished eating?
Have they given him his present?
Have you seen my keys anywhere?

We use **will** to make questions in the future simple.

Will you come later?
Will he do the shopping?
Will she go to university?
Will they arrive before ten?

Using modal verbs to make questions

The modal verbs in English are **can**, **could**, **may**, **might**, **must**, **ought**, **shall**, **will** and **would**. Many of them are used to make questions.

> **Can** you speak Polish?
> **Could** they hear me?
> **May** I see the letter?
> **Shall** we call the police?
> **Will** she be able to do it?
> **Would** they come without you?

We do not usually use **must** in questions in modern English. Instead, we say **Do I/we/they have to ... ?**, **Does he/she/it have to ... ?** .

> **Do we have to** buy a ticket?
> **Do the dogs have to** stay outside?
> **Does he have to** go to work?
> **Does it have to** be repaired?

Using WH- words to make questions

When you want to get a detailed answer, not just *yes* or *no*, you must use a WH- question. The words **who**, **whose**, **what**, **which**, **when**, **where**, **why** and **how** are used to form these questions.

> **Who** gave you the money?
> **Whose** shoes are those?
> **What** shall I do with these books?
> **Which** plates shall I use?
> **When** did you leave university?
> **Where** is Lucy?
> **Why** do they look so unhappy?
> **How** can I earn more money?

Using your voice to make questions

When you are speaking, you can often use the tone of your voice to make what you are saying into a question, especially if your question shows surprise, or if you want to make sure about something. To do this, the tone must rise at the end of the sentence.

> She's still not here?
> It's your birthday?
> You're really sure that you don't want any more to eat?
> I can take all these?

Short forms

In English, we often use short forms of words, for example **I'm** (I am), **he'll** (he will), **didn't** (did not). In conversation we almost always use these forms – it would sound strange to say the words in their full form. These forms can also be used in informal writing.

We use an apostrophe (') to represent the missing letters.

These are the short forms we use.

> **'m** = am
> **'s** = is *or* has
> **'re** = are
> **'ve** = have
> **'ll** = will
> **'d** = would *or* had

> **I'm** very happy.
> **They're** having a party.
> **We've** finished our work.
> **He'll** ring you later.

's can mean either **is** or **has**.

> **John's** busy at the moment. (= John is)
> **Here's** your coat. (= here is)
> **She's** seen it before. (= she has)
> **Who's** eaten the cake? (= who has)

'd can mean either **would** or **had**.

> **I'd** like a cup of tea. (= I would)
> He said **he'd** do it later. (= he would)
> **She'd** gone to the shops. (= she had)
> **They'd** lost their dog. (= they had)

Short forms in negatives

Short forms are also used for negatives made with the auxiliary verbs (be, have and do), and with modal verbs such as can, will and must.

These are the negative short forms made with auxiliary verbs.

be	have	do
isn't = is not	**haven't** = have not	**don't** = do not
aren't = are not	**hasn't** = has not	**doesn't** = does not
wasn't = was not	**hadn't** = had not	**didn't** = did not
weren't = were not		

> My house **isn't** far from here.
> We **weren't** doing anything wrong.
> I **haven't** been to America.
> She **hasn't** seen the movie.
> I **don't** know anything about it.
> They **didn't** like the food.

These are the common negative short forms made with modal verbs.

can't = cannot **couldn't** = could not	**won't** = will not **wouldn't** = would not	**mustn't** = must not **shouldn't** = should not

> You **can't** go inside the building.
> We **couldn't** find him.
> It **won't** rain today.
> She **wouldn't** help us.
> You **mustn't** stay too late.
> I **shouldn't** eat so much.

Countable and uncountable nouns

Countable nouns are the words for things that we can count. They have singular and plural forms. They can have **a** or **an** in front of them. If they are singular, they *must* have a word like **a**, **an**, **the** or **his** in front of them.

> She ate **an apple**.
> I sat on **the chair**.
> Where shall I put **my coat**?
> Would you like **a biscuit**?

Uncountable nouns are the words for things that cannot be counted. They cannot have **a** or **an** in front of them, and they do not have a plural form.

> I was filled with **happiness**.
> I asked her for some **advice**.
> Mix the **water** with the **flour**.
> We were enjoying the **sunshine**.

Here are some very common uncountable nouns.

advice	furniture	progress
air	happiness	safety
anger	homework	knowledge
beauty	information	money
behaviour	luggage	water
damage	meat	work

Be careful with uncountable nouns, because they may be countable in your own language. Remember that the verb that goes with them must be singular.

> The **meat was** not cooked properly.
> The **damage has** not been repaired.
> The **information** he gave us **was** correct.
> Her **behaviour upsets** everyone.

Some/any

You can use **some** and **any** with plural countable nouns and with uncountable nouns.

> I'd like **some potatoes**.
> I haven't got **any shoes**.
> We need to buy **some furniture**.
> Do you have **any milk**?

Many/a few

You can use **many** and **a few** with plural countable nouns but not with uncountable nouns.

> There aren't **many shops** in the village.
> I've never seen so **many aeroplanes!**
> There were only **a few sandwiches** left.
> We waited for **a few minutes**.

Much

You can use **much** with uncountable nouns but not with countable nouns.

> You've given me too **much rice**.
> I haven't got **much experience** of working in offices.

A lot of

You can use **a lot of** with plural countable nouns and with uncountable nouns.

> I ate **a lot of biscuits**.
> He has visited **a lot of countries**.
> She suffered **a lot of pain**.
> There was **a lot of laughter** at his suggestion.

Phrasal verbs

Phrasal verbs

Phrasal verbs such as **get up** and **come in** are very common in English. They are formed with a main verb with a particle (a preposition or an adverb). Here are some very common phrasal verbs which are useful to learn.

break down to stop working
> *The car broke down.*
> *Our washing machine broke down.*

call (someone) back to telephone someone in return for a call they made to you
> *I'll call you back.*
> *Could you call back later?*

calm down to become less upset or excited
> *Calm down and listen to me.*
> *We'd better give him a bit of time to calm down.*

cheer (someone) up to start feeling happier or to make someone feel happier
> *I bought her some flowers to cheer her up.*
> *We cheered up when we saw our lovely hotel.*

come in to enter a place
> *Come in and sit down.*
> *Everyone stood up when the teacher came in.*

do something up to fasten something
> *Mari did up the buttons on her jacket.*
> *He did his belt up.*

fall over If a person falls over, they fall to the ground, and if an object falls over, it falls onto its side
> *I tripped on a branch and fell over.*
> *I knocked the vase and it fell over.*

fill something in/out to write information in the spaces on a form
> *When you have filled in the form, send it to your employer.*
> *I had to fill out an application for a visa.*

find out (something) to learn the facts about something
> *I'll watch the next episode and find out what happens.*
> *I broke the window and I'm really worried that Mum will find out.*

get over something to become happy and well again after an unhappy experience or an illness
> *It took me a long time to get over her death.*
> *I can't go running until I get over this cold.*

get up to get out of bed
> *They have to get up early in the morning.*
> *I hate getting up!*

give in to agree to do something although you do not really want to do it
> *After saying 'no' a hundred times, I finally gave in and said 'yes'.*
> *We will not give in to their demands.*

give up to decide that you cannot do something and stop trying to do it
> *I give up I'll never understand this.*
> *She struggled to climb the mountain, but she never thought of giving up.*

give up something to stop doing or having something
> *I have decided to give up eating meat.*
> *I have had to give up swimming because of my skin problems.*

grow up to gradually change from being a child into being an adult.
> *She grew up in Shanghai.*
> *When he grows up, he wants to be a doctor.*

hurry up to do something more quickly
> *Hurry up and get ready or you'll miss the school bus.*
> *I need to hurry up and get this work finished.*

join in (something) to start to take part in an activity with other people
> *I started singing and everyone else joined in.*
> *He never joined in our discussions.*

keep on doing sth to continue to do something or to do something many times
> I asked them to be quiet, but they kept on talking.
> She kept on asking silly questions.

leave someone/something out to not include someone or something
> Why did they leave her out of the team?
> I made the cake, but I left out the cherries because I don't like them.

look after someone/something to take care of someone or something
> Maria looks after the children while I'm at work.
> Could you look after my plants when I go on holiday?

look forward to something to want something to happen because you think you will enjoy it
> She's looking forward to her holiday in Hawaii.
> I was looking forward to having a rest.

make something up to invent something
> It was all lies. I made it all up.
> We made up a new game.

pick someone/something up to collect someone or something from a place, often in a car
> Please could you pick me up at 5pm?
> She went to her parents' house to pick up some clean clothes.

put something away to put something back in the place where it is usually kept
> Kyle put the milk away in the fridge.
> I put away all the clean clothes.

put something on to place clothing on your body in order to wear it
> Grandma put her coat on and went out.
> I decided to put on my boots.

run out (of something) to have no more of something left
> We ran out of milk this morning.
> I need to get some more bread before we run out.

sit down to move your body down until you are sitting on something
>*Please sit down and make yourself comfortable.*
>*I sat down on the rock.*

take off used for saying that an aeroplane leaves the ground and starts flying
>*We took off at 11 o'clock.*
>*When did the plane take off?*

tell someone off to speak to someone in an angry or serious way because they have done something wrong
>*He never listened to us when we told him off.*
>*I told her off for being so rude.*

wake up to stop sleeping
>*I woke up early.*
>*What time do you normally wake up?*

wash (something) up to wash dishes
>*You cooked, so I'll wash up.*
>*Could you wash up the big pan for me?*